CHINESE HOME COOKING

CHINESE HOME COOKING

Julia Chih Cheng

Photographs
by
Yoshikatsu Saeki

KODANSHA INTERNATIONAL LTD.
Tokyo, New York & San Francisco

DISTRIBUTORS:

The UNITED STATES: Kodansha International/USA Ltd., through Harper & Row, Publishers, Inc., 10 East 53rd Street, New York, New York 10022. CANADA: Fitzhenry & Whiteside Ltd., 150 Lesmill Road, Don Mills, Ontario M3B 2T5. MEXICO & CENTRAL AMERICA: Harla S.A. de C.V., Apartado 30-546, Mexico 4, D.F. SOUTH AMERICA: Harper & Row, Publishers, Inc., International Department. UNITED KINGDOM: Phaidon Press Ltd., Unit B, Ridgeway Trading Estate, Iver, Bucks SL0 9HW. EUROPE: Boxerbooks, Inc., Limmatstrasse 111, 8031 Zurich. AUSTRALIA & NEW ZEALAND: Book Wise (Australia) Pty. Ltd., 104-8 Sussex Street, Sydney 2000. ASIA: Toppan Company (S) Pte. Ltd., 38 Liu Fang Road, Jurong Town, Singapore 2262.

Published by Kodansha International Ltd., 12-21, Otowa 2-chome, Bunkyo-ku, Tokyo 112 and Kodansha International/USA Ltd., 10 East 53rd Street, New York, New York 10022 and 44 Montgomery Street, San Francisco, California 94104. Copyright © 1972 by Kodansha International Ltd. All rights reserved. Printed in Japan.

LCC 79-174217
ISBN 0-87011-439-5
JBC 2077-789183-2361

First paperback edition, 1980

Contents

My Sister   by Nancy Chih Ma 7
This Book 9
Color Plates 13
Home Cooking
    Health and Beauty 39
    And the Kitchen Sink 40
    Styles and Places 40
    Utensils 41
    Ingredients 42
    Preparation 53
    Cooking 54
    Serving 55
    Menu 56

Recipes
- Poultry 59
- Fish 69
- Shellfish 73
- Beef 81
- Pork 85
- Vegetables 93
- Egg 103
- Rice, Noodles, and Bread 105
- Soups 120
- Desserts 125

List of Recipes 130

Index 133

My Sister

It is an old custom in China for a daughter to marry someone in the same province, mainly for the simple reasons that families in the same area know each other well, their habits are similar, and the bride can visit her home more easily if it is near. She can get help when it is needed, such as when she has a baby, becomes sick, or if her mother-in-law turns out to be stronger than she is.

However, despite the custom, my younger sister Julia was courted by and married a handsome young Cantonese man from Hong Kong. Although he is a prominent dentist and a fine gentleman with a big family, and although they were married over sixteen years ago, my mother still worries a little over how my sister is managing the different dialect and the daily food.

Since my sister moved to Hong Kong, of course our families have a kept in close touch and have exchanged visits many times. Her house is Western style, with two wings, has a garden with a fountain, and is surrounded by magnolias, willows, and tropical flowers. The entire house is furnished with Chinese furniture, and in the garden are Chinese porcelain stools and old Chinese vases as tall as I am. In this lovely home one can breathe the atmosphere of both East and West.

When visiting my sister, I always go to the kitchen to watch the women preparing Cantonese food. The differences between my native northern cooking are fascinating. For instance, it seems pans are almost always covered after stir-frying, and the leeks are so tiny that they are tied in a knot to make them easier to retrieve.

The large family meals are a constant pleasure. Counting all the in-laws, there are ten people in my sister's family, and every meal is a feast. But it is the Cantonese style, so different from my northern cooking, that attracts me most. Spareribs, steamed salt fish with eggs, stir-fried greens, barbecued pork, white cut chicken; all the food is fresh and wonderful.

After my sister moved to Hong Kong, she spent five years learning Cantonese cooking. Though she has several cooks at home, she finds some of her greatest pleasure working in the kitchen herself.

This, her book, has been born from the harmony of her family life and from her sweet, gentle nature. As we say in Chinese, love and peace will float from the words and lines to your kitchen and dining table.

Nancy Chih Ma

Tokyo, 1972

This Book

Somehow I have been attracted to cooking since I was little. Strangely enough, my brother and sister in Tokyo are both actively involved in the world of food. My sister's cookbooks have been translated into many languages, and my brother owns one of Tokyo's better supermarkets. Our father's cook, Chen, may have been at fault. I can still remember the wonderful meals—Chinese and Western—he prepared in our house in Harbin. But Chen was as taciturn as he was skilled: he never welcomed the girls to the kitchen and he never divulged his secrets.

My relatives were not so reluctant, and I eventually learned the cooking of my native North China. After I married in Tokyo and moved to Hong Kong, the buns, breads, and noodles of the North were a great novelty to my Cantonese family and friends, and I occasionally treated them to northern cooking parties. What happened next was natural—for five years I filled my time with the pleasures of discovering, researching, and learning the world of Cantonese food. Then my repertoire increased to much more than northern dishes to please my husband and family. And I came to understand the meaning of the Chinese proverb, "When you eat, eat in Canton."

All this time, my sister Nancy was giving cooking classes in Tokyo. Then she opened her own restaurant, started to publish books, traveled around the world, and appeared on television in many American cities. The family was both astonished and delighted. This summer I visited my family and eighty-five-year-old mother in Tokyo, before moving to the United States with my husband. My little mother was full of stories of the food on the farm in North China where she grew up. Is it the food that has given her long life? This thought plus the many talks with my sister and hearing the comments of customers in her restaurant and seeing my nieces, who also are accomplished cooks and teach cooking—these gave me that little bit of extra courage when my sister suddenly proposed that I, too, do a cookbook. The people at Kodansha International said yes, and this little book was conceived.

I, as the youngest daughter of a big Chinese family, am expected to be weepy and sentimental. This must be true, for I have no compunctions about admitting that I get a warm and rewarding feeling just visualizing your family and friends enjoying the dishes made from these recipes.

A harmonious life is nourished by delicious food. Blending flavors and matching tastes is not enough without the addition of love, and love is not an ingredient—it is you, and it is what makes a cook an artist.

Julia Chih Cheng

Tokyo and Hong Kong, 1972

Preparing a feast is easy, but inviting guests is difficult; inviting guests is easy, but good hospitality is difficult.

弁洒不難請客難，請客不難欵客難

Cold Lobster, Braised Mushrooms with Asparagus, Cold Cut Arrangement, Sweet and Sour Fish

Ground Beef with Green Peas, Jellied Chicken, Steamed Stuffed Green Peppers, Spicy Shrimp, Skewered Chicken Livers

Chopped Chicken with Lettuce, Duck with Chinese Cabbage,
Pickled Red Radishes, Marinated Cucumber, Chili Turnips

Steamed Salmon with Eggs, Braised Chicken with Black Bean Sauce, Chicken Breast with Pineapple, Pork with Plums

Beauty in Bloom, Braised Duck with Onions, Fried Crab Claws, Beancurd with Oyster Sauce, Stir-Fried Pork with Pickles

Corn Soup with Ground Chicken, Fried Duck, Fried Stuffed Eggplant, Shrimp with Celery

Deep Fried Eggs, Lemon Chicken, Jellyfish and Cucumber

Beef in Yunnan Pot, Fried Oysters with Asparagus, Stir-Fried Cuttlefish

Steamed Fish, Steamed Wintermelon with Ham, Two-Color Shrimp Balls

Sweet and Sour Prawns, Chicken with Chestnuts, Corn Fritters, Stuffed Mushrooms with Sausage

Fried Chicken (whole), Barbecued Spareribs, Spicy Assorted Vegetables

Beef with Shredded Potatoes, Braised Assorted Vegetables, Drunk Chicken, Braised Spareribs

Pork with String Beans, Chinese Beef Steak, Steamed Chicken with Ham, Scallops and Chicken Livers with Celery

Fried Wonton, Beef with Broccoli, Sautéed Beancurd with Mushrooms, Crab with Black Bean Sauce

Chinese Cabbage and Mushroom Soup, Pork with Cucumber, Green Peppers and Bean Sprouts, Sweet and Sour Pork Strips, Forest Eggs

Fried Chicken (pieces), Stir-Fried Beef with Snow Peas, Assorted Vegetables with Black Pickles, Fried Rice with Assorted Meat, Fried Shrimp, Sautéed Chicken Livers with Celery

Barbecued Pork, Chilled Cucumber, Anise Braised Beef, White Chicken, Spiced Fish Slices, Fried Pork; on tray: Sausage, Spicy Salad, Spicy Lima Beans, Crisp Peanuts

Cantonese Firepot

Watercress Soup, Longevity Chicken, Shrimp Ball Soup, Sesame Shrimp Toast

Braised Fish with Beancurd, Crisp Fried Noodles with Spinach, Soft Fried Noodles with Shrimp, Clam Soup

Steamed Dumplings, Scrambled Eggs with Crabmeat, Fried Dumplings, Sweet and Sour Pork, Chicken with Walnuts, Egg Noodles with Shrimp, Spinach Noodles with Chicken

Shrimp Dumplings, Steamed Flower Buns, Steamed Silver Strand Rolls, Spring Rolls, Abalone and Chicken Congee

Glazed Sweet Potatoes, Fruit Compote, Stuffed Sweet Lotus, Stuffed Apples

Sesame Puffs (on tray with oranges and loquats), Almond Float, Longan and Lichee Compote, Sweet Red Beans with Gingko Nuts

The best meat makes the best soup.

好肉出好湯

HOME COOKING

Chinese cooking has become one of the international culinary languages. But until rather recently, Chinese food has always meant "eating out." Perhaps this is because many of the ingredients were once hard to obtain, and preparation seemed exotic and difficult. The primary ingredients are now either readily available or substitutions can be made. And anyone with a good, sharp kitchen knife and a deep, thick frying pan can do the preparation.

Health and Beauty

Many people have come to realize that Chinese food is truly a food for health and a naturally trim waistline. Most of the preparation time is for cutting and blending ingredients; the actual cooking time, especially for vegetables, is very short, and the result is incomparable freshness. Cooking on a high heat seals in flavor and vitamins. Though frying is the most common cooking method, all oils are light, vegetable products, and the brief cooking time with constant stirring insures that no foods get soggy and overdone. One of the main themes in Chinese cooking is capturing and holding the natural color, texture, aroma, and nourishment of all food.

Smaller portions of a larger number of dishes at one sitting allow a leisurely meal with a variety of balanced foods and flavors and leave no feeling of heaviness. Though many people are adroit indeed with chopsticks, there is a practical limit to the amount of food that can

HOME COOKING

be picked up at one time. The ingredients of Chinese food are thus cut small, which also aids the digestion. Though possible, it is not practical to attack a slab of prime rib and a baked potato with chopsticks.

I enjoy the food of all countries, but my everyday meals are of course Chinese. For the reasons given here, and because I can still (at over forty) wear the same dress size as my lovely young niece Helen (on the left in the inside front jacket photo), I am convinced that Chinese cooking is the healthiest. It is not necessary to include medicinal herbs in recipes (see Longevity Chicken, p. 68) to benefit from a daily dose of delicious and nourishing Chinese food made in your own kitchen. Thus one reason for writing this book.

And the Kitchen Sink

Like all good cooking, improvisation is basic to Chinese food, and new dishes or variations are always being invented. With a few basic seasonings, Chinese dishes can be made from almost any combination of ingredients. It is with this idea that the basic seasoning combinations and marinades are clearly set off in the recipes here. A brief glance at the kinds of seasonings, their proportions, and the way they are combined and used should give anyone the basic idea and let the imagination go free and fanciful in this world of Chinese home cooking.

Styles and Places

The idea that Chinese cooking is like a language is very appropriate to the different styles of cooking too, because this huge country has many local "dialects" of food. I just want to lead up to the point that the recipes here are Cantonese, which is the kind of food I make for my husband and family. Most readers have at least some favorite Cantonese dishes, since the majority of the Chinese restaurants outside of China are Cantonese. But there are so many dishes and so many variations in the regional styles of cooking that I doubt even the fanciest restaurant carries a large portion of the recipes in this book on its menu.

Chinese regional styles vary for the most part in the spices and seasonings they use, in their emphasis on certain local products, and in their preference for certain cooking methods. Kwangtung (Canton) historically has seen waves of immigration from other parts of China. Cantonese cooking took form sometime in the seventeenth century, which is very recent indeed in the history of China. Based on the cuisine brought south from the imperial capital of Peking, Cantonese food became famous for its rich variety, delicacy, emphasis on natural flavor, steamed and roast meat and poultry, and its use of the harvest of the South China Sea, including such famous delicacies as shark's fins and bird's nest soup. Natural flavors are best preserved by quick cooking, and Cantonese food is noted for having developed to a fine art the technique of stir-frying.

HOME COOKING

Utensils

It would be defeating the purpose of this book to say that such and such utensils are necessary and indispensable to cook Chinese food. Miracles can be cooked with the pots, pans, knives, etc. found in Western kitchens. But the utensils that developed with and for Chinese cooking are the best tools for the job. As the cook finds how easy and delicious Chinese food is when made at home, choosing and buying Chinese cooking utensils becomes the next natural step. Some utensils, like the steamer, are rather specialized, but the *wok* skillet might just become the most used pan in the kitchen, and the small Chinese cleaver is the most versatile kitchen knife I know.

knives: Since most of the time in the kitchen is spent cutting and otherwise preparing ingredients for cooking, a good sharp knife is the cook's right hand. The little Chinese cleaver pictured on page 49, though it may look clumsy, is an all-purpose knife that can do everything from shaving paper-thin radish flowers to chopping—bones and all—bite-sized pieces of a tough, old boiler hen. Whatever knife is used, it should be a friend, companion, sage, and poet in the kitchen. And to give the knife its full power of expression, it must be kept sharp!

The variety of Chinese knives is large, but most are used for special purposes by professional cooks. Besides the cleaver, an ordinary, pointed fruit knife is handy in the kitchen for fine work. Both Chinese and Japanese supply stores should stock a good selection of knives. Stainless knives are convenient but dull quickly and are hard to sharpen; tempered steel knives are easier to keep sharp, and the problem of rusting can be solved simply by drying them thoroughly after each use, wrapping the blade in wax paper when not in use, and rubbing them occasionally with a bit of vegetable oil.

cutting board: The Chinese cutting board is a six-inch-thick slice of a hardwood tree truck (see photo, p. 49). This is by far the most easily used cutting board and chopping block, but it may pose a storage problem in a small kitchen. Any good hardwood cutting board will do. The board should be large enough to hold an ample volume of chopped ingredients and should be as thick as possible.

pans: A thick, deep, twelve or fourteen-inch frying pan and a lid to fit are satisfactory, although a good, thick saucepan may also be used, even for stir-frying. The *wok* frying pan (see photo, p. 49), however, cannot be overpraised. The wok is such a versatile utensil that it is well worth the small cost, and may turn out to be indispensable for all cooking, not just Chinese. Its round shape lets the heat distribute evenly for excellent frying, and provides ample depth for boiling and simmering (stews and spaghetti sauce) and deep frying as well. Filled with a few inches of boiling water, it can be used to provide steam for the Chinese steamer (see photo, p. 49), or an excellent steamer can be made by placing a plate or bowl on a round wire rack above the boiling water and covering appropriately.

HOME COOKING

Like a good iron skillet, the wok should be well seasoned. For electric and some gas ranges, a supporting ring is necessary to hold the round bottom.

A perforated strainer (photo, p. 49) that fits inside the wok may be very useful for deep frying. The spatula (photo, p. 49) used with the wok should have rounded corners for ease of use with the round contour of the pan. A slotted spoon (photo, p. 128) or wire-mesh dipper (not pictured) is also handy when deep frying.

steamer: Chinese steamers, of either bamboo (photo, p. 49; color, pp. 33, 34) or metal, can be stacked in tiers above the boiling water, thus making it possible to steam a number of foods at once. The advantages of this are obvious, but an excellent steamer for small ingredients can be improvised by placing a plate on a round, legged rack or on a bowl in a large pot with a close-fitting lid. The water level should be at least two inches below the plate, and the plate should not touch the sides of the pot. It is important that the boiling water should not touch the food, and that the steam should circulate freely. To steam poultry whole, the bird may be placed in a bowl, and the bowl then placed in a covered pot with boiling water; the boiling water level should be kept between one-half and two-thirds the height of the bowl.

Ingredients

The photograph on page 50 shows some of the ingredients used in the recipes here that might be unfamiliar to the shopper. Since many of the ingredients used in Japanese cooking are identical with or extremely close to the Chinese, in cases where an ingredient should be available in Japanese foodshops, the Japanese name is also given to help the shopper.

There seems to be no standard English term for many ingredients, and different cookbooks use different terms for the same thing. Just in case, then, that the Chinese grocer or local restaurant might not understand what you are asking for, the Chinese characters for all the special things are included. (But the romanized Japanese words only are given.) My publishers have assured me that this book is planned to be very portable and can be easily carried to the grocer to show him the appropriate Chinese characters for the foods you wish to buy.

agar-agar: (洋粉; Japanese: *kanten*). A delicate, flavorless jelly processed from a special seaweed. Comes in packaged stick (photo, p. 50) or thread form. Should be washed, soaked in water until soft, squeezed out, and dissolved in boiling liquid. The exact proportions will depend on the firmness of the jelly desired. A finer textured, more delicate confection can be made than with gelatin, and agar-agar does not have the rubbery quality of the latter, though gelatin is the only convenient substitute. A strong solution of agar-agar will start to set at room temperature, so care should be taken when mixing it with other ingredients.

anise, star: (茴香). A brown, eight-pointed seed pod (photo, p. 50), resembling conventional aniseed, but with a pleasant bitterness and not so licoricelike flavor. Used to flavor meats and steamed poultry. Conventionally used in conjunction with anise pepper, but the difficulty of obtaining the latter has resulted in star anise being used alone. One-third tsp. powdered star anise is approximately equivalent to one whole clove. Available powdered or whole in Oriental foodshops and in the spice section of well-stocked supermarkets.

bamboo shoots: (筍; Japanese: *take no ko*). Fresh bamboo shoots (photo, p. 50) are of course more delicious than canned, but the fresh are difficult to find and are expensive. The canned form is available in all well-stocked markets. Canned shoots need only be drained and rinsed before using; fresh shoots (already husked) should be parboiled.

beancurd: (豆腐; Japanese: *tōfu*). This versatile and nutritious food is familiar to anyone who has enjoyed Chinese or Japanese food. It is usually sold in cakes, but also comes canned. I was a bit perplexed when told that beancurd cakes vary in size somewhat between Chinese and Japanese foodstores, and even between different areas of the United States. Because of the delicate flavor of this food and because beancurd is so versatile, there is no problem in specifying "one cake" of this ingredient in the recipes here. It is very doubtful that it will be necessary, but the cook can easily compensate if the amount of beancurd specified seems too large or too small. Available fresh in Oriental foodshops and often in the produce departments of supermarkets.

bean sprouts: (豆芽菜; Japanese: *moyashi*). Ordinary bean sprouts are the sprouts of mung beans (photo, p. 50); the larger variety are the sprouts of soy beans. Take care to keep the crisp freshness of the succulent sprouts by cooking only a minimum time. Bean sprouts quickly become soggy if overcooked, and dominate other flavors. Canned bean sprouts should be rinsed, then crisped in cold water in the refrigerator for at least an hour. To grow your own: soak $\frac{1}{4}$ lb. mung beans (or soy beans) in warm water overnight. Place a large collander in a roasting pan or dishpan (to catch runoff water), and line collander with 2-3 layers cheesecloth. Dampen cheesecloth with warm water, spread beans in an even layer over cheesecloth, and cover with another double layer of cloth dampened in warm water. Place collander in a totally dark place (or the sprouts will not be white), and keep beans warm and damp until sprouts mature (4 days for 1-inch mung bean sprouts; 5 days for 2-inch soy bean sprouts). Maturing time depends on the temperature; an average temperature of 72° F. is ideal. Sprinkle cheesecloth with warm water at regular intervals. One-fourth pound of beans yields more than 1 pound of sprouts. Wash in ample water before using.

HOME COOKING

beans, black fermented: (豆豉). These small, pungent, salt-preserved beans (photo, p. 50) are used to highlight the flavors of meat and seafood and to make rich sauces. Available canned or in bulk. Fermented beans may be soaked beforehand in hot water for about 10 minutes and added to the other ingredients with or without the soaking water, depending on the strength of flavor desired. Do not overuse; a small can or plastic bag of beans lasts a long time.

beans, red: (豆沙; Japanese: *azuki*). Available dried or already sweetened in cans. The sweetened preparation is sold in Japanese foodshops and can be used directly from the can. Take care to buy the whole sweetened beans and not the smooth, strained confection.

cabbage, Chinese: (白菜; Japanese: *hakusai*). Available fresh (photo, p. 50) in Oriental foodshops. Chinese cabbage overcooks easily, and care should be taken to keep it crisp and fresh when stir-frying. Can be combined with anything.

eggplant: (茄子, Japanese: *nasu*). The Oriental eggplant is smaller (photo, p. 50) and more delicate in flavor and texture than the large, Western variety. If these small eggplants are available, they should by all means be used in the recipes here.

eggs, quail: (鶉鶉蛋; Japanese: *uzura no tamago*). These small, speckled eggs (photo, p. 50) do not differ much in flavor from chicken eggs, and bantam-size chicken eggs may be substituted.

five-flavor spice: (五香粉). This fragrant spice mixture is sold bottled or by weight. It is composed of 3 parts each of powdered star anise, anise pepper (Japanese: *sanshō*), and cinnamon to two parts each of fennel and cloves. Used (sparingly) with meat and poultry. Allspice or a mixture of equal portions of powdered cinnamon, cloves, aniseed, and thyme may be substituted.

flour, glutinous rice: (糯米粉; Japanese: *shiratamako*). This flour is used mainly for sweet confections, and is readily available in Chinese and Japanese foodshops.

ginger, fresh: (姜; Japanese: *shōga*). Though both powdered and dried ginger are easily available, the fresh root (photo, p. 50) should be used if possible. Unless specified otherwise, the skin should be removed. Slices should be about $\frac{1}{8}$-inch thick. Ginger juice can be made by crushing pieces of the fresh root in a garlic press. One tsp. grated fresh ginger is equivalent to $\frac{1}{8}$ tsp. powdered ginger. Dried ginger is much better than the powdered form; the dried root should be soaked for 2 or more hours and used in slightly smaller quantities than the fresh.

gingko nuts: (白果; Japanese: *ginnan*). Available fresh or canned (photo, p. 50). The fresh should be shelled, blanched by boiling about 10 minutes, and the thin inner skin removed. The canned nuts should be rinsed before using.

hoisin sauce: (海鮮醬). A sweet, spicy sauce used largely for pork and poultry and also as a condiment. Available canned (photo, p. 50) or bottled. Lends itself well as a barbecue sauce.

jellyfish, dried: (海蜇皮). Jellyfish, cured with salt and alum and dried, comes in sheets or rolls (photo, p. 50). Wash jellyfish in water and soak overnight (if thin) or for 3 days (if thick) in cold water, changing water every day. Drain, and rinse thoroughly and quickly in hot (not boiling) water. Shred just the amount required by folding in layers and cutting across layers in thin strips (like noodles, p. 110). Wash and drain again. Remaining jellyfish may be kept in water for up to two weeks if the water is changed every day. Available in Chinese foodstores.

leek: (葱; Japanese: *negi*). The Oriental leek resembles a giant green onion with a straight stalk and a long white part (photo, p. 50). Spanish onions, of course, may be substituted, though the slight bitterness of the leek is preferred for some dishes. Finely chopped leek is used widely as a seasoning in the Orient. Available in both Chinese and Japanese foodstores.

lichee: (荔枝). This fruit is available fresh, frozen, canned, and dried (photo, p. 50). The fresh and frozen are hard to find and expensive. The canned form is preserved in light syrup and is the most convenient for the recipes here. Sold in Chinese foodshops and well-stocked supermarkets.

lily roots: (百合). Sold fresh or canned in Chinese foodshops. Probably hard to find, however, and diced sweet chestnuts may be substituted.

longan: (龍眼). Similar to the lichee, and also available fresh, frozen, canned, or dried (photo, p. 50). Only the dried is used here, and is sold in Chinese foodshops.

lotus root: (藕; Japanese: *renkon*). The slightly sweet flavor and crunchy texture of lotus root gives it wide use as a vegetable. Sliced, it can be added to various stir-fried vegetables and meat as well as boiled dishes. Available fresh (photo, p. 50; it grows in 5-8 inch plump links, like a sausage) or canned, and is sold in both Chinese and Japanese foodshops.

lotus seeds: (蓮子; Japanese: *hasu no mi*). It is doubtful that the fresh seeds are available in the U.S., but canned seeds should be sold in Chinese foodshops. Blanched almonds, whole or roughly slivered, may be substituted.

mushrooms, dried Chinese: (冬菇; Japanese: *hoshi shiitake*). Brown Chinese mushrooms are one case in which the dried form (photo, p. 50) is the tastiest and best for cooking, especially in stir-fried and boiled dishes, though the delicacy of fresh mushrooms (photo, p. 50) is often the most appropriate for certain dishes. The dried mushrooms should be soaked in lukewarm water until soft (about 20 minutes), the stems removed (stems may be used in making stock), and then cut appropriately. Fresh mushrooms should also be stemmed. The dried variety should not be overused in any

HOME COOKING

one recipe. Dried Italian mushrooms may be substituted, but white champignons are not a substitute.

mushrooms, cloud ear: (木耳; Japanese: *kikurage*). Many people wrinkle their nose at the idea of eating a tree fungus, but earth fungi (truffles) are a famous French delicacy. The crunchy, slightly gelatinous texture and delicate flavor of cloud ear mushrooms enhance a wide variety of dishes in Chinese cooking. These mushrooms are sold dried (photo, p. 50), and should be washed, soaked in warm water until soft (at least 15 minutes), have the hard parts discarded, be rinsed again, and drained. They will expand about five times in volume. Available mainly in Chinese foodstores.

noodles, dried Chinese: (麵條; Japanese: *ramen*). Both Chinese egg and wheat noodles come in dried, packaged form and are available in Chinese and Japanese foodstores, as well as in supermarkets. Many supermarkets now also sell Japanese instant noodles, which are adequate, but not as good as the unprepared dried form, which in turn are not as good as the homemade. Noodles, common and simple and taken for granted, can become glorious if made at home. Western noodles are not a good substitute.

oil: (油). Important! Do not use animal fats or oils, do not use olive oil or anything else fancy. Never use shortening for frying Chinese food. A clear, light liquid, flavorless vegetable oil, unless otherwise specified, allows the flavors of foods to come out naturally and allows dishes to be eaten cold without tasting greasy. Peanut oil or corn oil is ideal; either can be heated to high temperatures without burning and can be reused many times simply by browning $\frac{1}{2}$ stalk leek and 2–3 slices ginger in the oil before use.

oil, red pepper: (辣油). Sold in small bottles in Chinese foodstores. Used as a seasoning for dips, usually in combination with soy sauce, and in stir-frying. Red pepper oil may be added whenever a bit of chili flavor will liven a dish, but use sparingly. To make: mix 1 part red chili pepper flakes or powder (do not use commercial chili powder, which is a blend of spices) with 4 parts sesame oil, and simmer (uncovered) until pepper turns brown. Strain into bottles.

oil, sesame: (芝麻油; Japanese: *goma abura*). An important seasoning in Chinese and Japanese food, and a basic ingredient in Korean cooking. This amber-colored oil is never used in large quantities, except perhaps to mix with vegetable oil in certain deep fried dishes. Though slightly costly, a small bottle will last a long time. The nutlike flavor, though not strong, is distinct; do not overuse.

oyster sauce: (蠔油). A rich sauce made by a complicated process from oysters, soy sauce, etc. Used as a seasoning and in sauces; has wider uses than hoisin sauce and is excellent for Western cooking, especially meats. Sold canned (photo, p. 50) or bottled in Chinese foodstores.

pepper, anise: (花椒; Japanese: *sanshō*). An aromatic, pungent, small seed pod (photo, p. 50), reddish brown in color and somewhat pepperlike in flavor, but with a distinct taste of its own. Almost always used in conjunction with star anise in flavoring meats and in steaming to reduce the strong overtones of duck, pork, etc. Usually anise pepper is ground and mixed with salt to provide a dip for duck and other fatty foods, but conventional black pepper has become a convenient and good substitute. Anise pepper is not included in the recipes here, but if you do decide to use it in conjunction with star anise, use it sparingly. The powdered form comes bottled, and the whole pods are sold in bulk; should be available in both Chinese and Japanese foodshops.

pepper, red chili: (紅辣椒; Japanese: *tōgarashi*). The small, dried red chilies are used in Chinese cooking, and the flaked, rather than the powdered, form is preferred, unless otherwise specified. If any substitutions are made, such as Tabasco sauce, chili powder, or hot canned or bottled chilies, care should be taken not to overdo this volatile spice.

pepper-salt mixture: (花椒塩). Toast whole black peppercorns over high heat in a dry frying pan until they begin to crackle. Remove from heat and grind (with mortar and pestle preferably) to a medium rough grind. Mix with salt in proportions of 1 : 1 or 3 salt : 2 pepper.

plums, preserved: (話梅). These complex-flavored, dried plums (or apricots) are sold in Chinese food and confection shops. They are a pinkish or reddish brown in color, are sold either in bulk or in cellophane bags, and are often individually wrapped, like candy. They are usually eaten as a confection and as a mouth sweetener after or between meals, but when steamed with meat they provide a delicious and unusual flavor background. Japanese medium-sized, soft, brine-preserved plums (*umeboshi*) (photo, p. 50) may be substituted, but the flavor is different.

rice: (米). Cantonese meals are accompanied by rice, though it is by no means mandatory. Long grain rice is preferred, and can be boiled, steamed, or both. Follow directions on package.

rice, glutinous: (糯米; Japanese: *mochi-gome*). A short-grained, sticky variety of rice used mostly in confections. Widely available in both Chinese and Japanese stores. Preparation: wash rice until water runs clear, then soak 30 minutes in cold water, and drain. Place rice in a thick saucepan, add the same volume of water as rice, cover, and bring to a quick boil. Immediately reduce heat to low, and cook until water is completely absorbed (about 30 minutes for 1 cup rice). Do not remove pot cover while cooking.

rose wine, Chinese: (玫瑰酒). If you are lucky enough to find this rather strong but very pleasant liquor (it is not sweet), you may prefer to use it for drinking rather than for cooking. Unfortunately, at the time of writing I have no hints as to where it can be obtained in the United States.

HOME COOKING

soup stock: (鷄湯). Chicken stock is used in Cantonese cooking and can be made in three ways. 1) Cover a boiler hen with water plus two inches extra. Simmer with 1 stalk leek and 4 slices ginger for 1½–2 hours. 2) If a spring chicken is used, simmer with leek and ginger for 30 minutes. 3) Simmer the bones of 2 chickens with leek and ginger for 1 hour. If only a small quantity of stock is required, chicken bouillon cubes may be used.

soy sauce: (醬油; Japanese: *shōyu*). Japanese soy sauce should be available now in almost all supermarkets, and is excellent for all but very special uses. The thick, salty, and bitter domestically made American stuff advertised as soy sauce should be diluted to half strength if used. If a good, Oriental soy sauce is not available nearby, take the trouble to get a healthy-sized can or bottle the next time you shop where it is available. Like salt, its uses are limitless.

vermicelli, transparent: (粉糸). These are also called transparent noodles, and are fine, white threads made from ground mung beans. They are sold in Chinese foodshops in dried form, and should be soaked in lukewarm water until soft before being added to stir-fried or boiled dishes. Do not overcook, or the filaments will expand and become starchy. Japanese *harusame* is an adequate substitute, but Italian vermicelli is not.

water chestnuts: (荸薺; Japanese: *kuwai*). Available fresh or canned (photo, p. 50), these succulent and crunchy bulbs are a versatile vegetable that can be added to many stir-fried dishes and also to soups and even desserts (see p. 126). The canned form is the easiest to use and is available in Chinese foodshops and well-stocked supermarkets.

wine: (酒). Chinese wine is a basic seasoning for most Chinese cooking. Dry sherry is specified here as a substitute. Avoid cooking sherry or cream sherry. An even better substitute, however, is Japanese saké, which is close to the Chinese original. Other light, white wines, and even gin, may be used. Inexpensive Japanese saké should be almost universally available in American liquor stores, and if not, can be easily ordered.

wintermelon: (冬瓜; Japanese: *tōgan*). This delicately flavored melon has a very white meat and a tough, green skin (photo, p. 50), often with a frosty white coating. Can be used in many steamed dishes, and is used in soups. Take care not to overcook.

HOME COOKING

1. cleaver and chopping board

2. wok, frying strainer, and spatula

3. steamer

HOME COOKING

4. ingredients:

1. lotus root
2. leek
3. wintermelon
4. dried jellyfish
5. oyster sauce
6. hoisin sauce
7. fresh ginger
8. Chinese cabbage
9. dried agar-agar
10. star anise
11. red chili peppers
12. bean sprouts
13. transparent vermicelli
14. eggplant
15. dried Chinese mushrooms
16. fermented black beans
17. anise pepper
18. dried lichees
19. preserved plums
20. dried cloud ear mushrooms
21. fresh Chinese mushrooms
22. black turnip pickles
23. quail eggs
24. canned gingko nuts
25. dried longans
26. canned water chestnuts
27. walnuts
28. bamboo shoot
29. *chün shan* wafers
30. *kou tzu* seeds

HOME COOKING

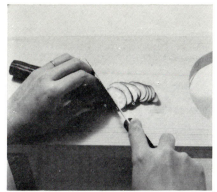 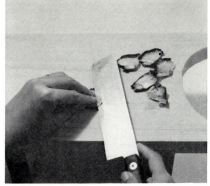 

5. slicing I   6. slicing II   7. shredding

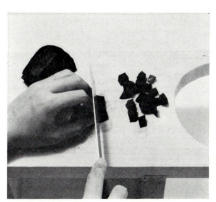 

8. dicing   9. fine chopping

HOME COOKING

10. wedging

11–13. scoring

12.

13.

Preparation

The main hint to give about preparing ingredients for Chinese cooking is the various ways of cutting. The basic basics are illustrated on page 51; from there you can start getting fancy. But even some of the basic cutting methods are not always necessary. Young people always seem in a hurry, and my niece Helen, without a worry, combines whole this and whole that with the right seasonings, stir-fries the mixture, and makes delicious dishes. She wants to write a book titled something like "Crazy Chinese Cooking," and it probably will be a huge success. But the point is that Chinese cooking has a few simple rules, and before they can be broken, the cook should know what they are. Then you are completely free to do what you want.

The four basic cutting techniques for Chinese cooking are slicing, shredding, dicing, and fine chopping (mincing). Wedging and scoring are helpful variations.

There is no mystique about cutting, though watching a professional Chinese cook is awe inspiring and can give you a good idea of the beautiful forms this art can take. The method of cooking and the natural size of any main ingredient determine the size of the other ingredients that need cutting. For stir-fried dishes, ingredients are cut small. For deep frying, chunks cook best. Steaming allows a greater flexibility, but nothing should be too thick. The other principle is that, for any given dish, all ingredients should be approximately the same size. There is ample variation on this principle; a glance at the color plates here will give a good idea of the leeway possible. The main exception to keeping the size of ingredients in one dish uniform is when a secondary vegetable is cut smaller than the main ingredients to give a color effect.

slicing: Diagonal slicing is the rule, but has exceptions. Especially with meat, which should be sliced perpendicularly to the grain. For stir-frying, ingredients (especially tender vegetables) should be sliced thin.

shredding: Shredding *does not mean grating* but means cutting into threadlike strips 1 to 2 inches long. This cutting method is almost always used for stir-frying. Occasionally a larger shred size is used for steaming or crisp deep frying.

dicing: The easiest way to cut an ingredient into little cubes is to first cut it into strips and then to cut across the strips. Used for stir-frying.

fine chopping (mincing): There are many ways to mince, but, generally, first shred the ingredient, then cut across the shreds, then, using the point of the knife as a fulcrum against the cutting board, chop quickly while feeding the mass of fine ingredient under the moving blade (or the knife may be held horizontally and brought down in small, swift cuts across the mass of fine ingredient, changing direction each time the mass is cut). Repeat the latter process until the desired fineness is obtained.

Meat and some other ingredients may be minced in

HOME COOKING

a meat grinder, but juices and tenderness are lost. It is worth the difference in flavor to finely chop meat by hand, and by the time the meat grinder is washed, there is not much time lost.

wedging: Ingredients are cut into triangular chunks about 1–1½ inches long. Used with tougher ingredients mainly for stir-frying, steaming, and boiling.

scoring: Cuttlefish and liver stir-fry most successfully if first cross-hatched diagonally with light, closely spaced incisions before being cut into 2-inch squares, then parboiled (if necessary), and stir-fried.

A point about preparation that cannot be overemphasized is to have all the seasonings and ingredients prepared and ready before cooking. Cooking times are fast and precise, and while the cook might be looking for the sesame oil on the kitchen shelf, the food in the frying pan may cook itself beyond palatability or expire entirely.

Cooking

The first time a cook tries to coordinate an entire Chinese meal with four or more dishes, she may feel like a combination of ballet dancer, acrobat, and Olympic sprinter. Breathless exertion, even when attempting to coordinate three or more stir-fried dishes simultaneously and get them on the table hot, is not necessary. Be casual. First plan the menu so that timings do not conflict. Second, prepare everything in advance, including mixing liquid and other seasonings and the cornstarch-water mixture. The best way is to first cook a few recipes as main courses in Western meals to get the feel of the timing. Then everything will be easy.

stir-frying: Dry heat the wok or frying pan over high heat until a drop of water sputters immediately, then add the oil. Heat the oil until it roils and a slight haze forms above the surface (but do not let it smoke). Then follow recipe directions. As the term indicates, stir-frying involves stirring the ingredients vigorously while cooking in oil over a high heat.

The usual order of stir-frying ingredients after the oil has been heated is: 1) add solid seasonings such as garlic, leek, ginger, fermented black beans; 2) add meat, precooked or raw, which should be cooked briefly, just until it changes color, before adding 3) salt and liquid seasonings, and then 4) vegetables, after which 5) water or soup stock is added, and finally 6) the cornstarch mixture. Often the meat is deep fried or stir-fried separately and added after the vegetables. There are any number of exceptions and variations to this order, but this is the basic pattern and will allow you to take off and try creating your own original stir-fried dishes.

Stir-fried dishes should be served immediately. If two or more stir-fried dishes are to be served, prepare the ingredients ahead of time so that as soon as one is finished, the other can be cooked immediately. The small wait while the other dishes are being cooked will not affect the freshness of the first dish.

HOME COOKING

deep frying: As a rule, deep frying oil is heated until hot (360°), and frying time is kept to a minimum. Where ingredients are delicate or a longer frying time is required, the recipes here specify the lower oil temperatures.

Vegetable oil can be reused many times if ½ stalk leek and 2–3 slices ginger are browned in the hot oil before use. Fish, however, tends to flavor the oil and limit its use only to fish. Since oil darkens with repeated use, delicate, white batter-coated foods require new oil.

steaming: Start with boiling water. Do not place the food over cold water and then bring it to a boil. If you own a Chinese steamer, adding more boiling water if necessary while steaming is not a problem, but if you make your own steamer from a large, covered pot into which a rack is set to hold a plate or bowl above the boiling water, be very careful to pour additional boiling water down the sides of the pot so that it does not touch the cooking ingredients. High heat is used for steaming, unless otherwise specified. When removing food from an improvised steamer, take the lid off and let the steam disperse a few minutes before removing the plate or bowl with a potholder.

Serving

Serving Chinese dishes as main courses in a Western meal is easy enough. To serve an entire Chinese meal is also easy. Even if you do not use chopsticks (why not try?), a little special attention to serving bowls and place settings is both fun and enlivens the atmosphere of the meal—and makes the food taste better as well.

For serving bowls, anything can be used as long as the food looks appropriate and attractive. The dishes, bowls, and trays used in the color photos here are from China, Japan, Korea, Okinawa, and I don't know where (the horn spoons were said to be Eskimo). Some are antiques, some new. The materials vary from folk pottery, to lacquer, to pewter, to plastic. Many of the tablecloths in the photos are antique Japanese quilt covers. The point is that whatever serving bowls are used, they should fit the food, but do not have to look Chinese. Plain white porcelain is excellent; elegant and flowery French chinaware would not be appropriate.

Though in many American Chinese restaurants everyone helps himself directly from the serving bowls with his own chopsticks and only has a rice bowl to hold the food, it is perfectly correct and much more convenient to put serving spoons in all the serving bowls and allow each diner to serve himself directly onto a plate.

It is nice to have a complete set of Chinese dishes, but it is not necessary. The approximately correct sizes given below for the various dishes in a place setting, however, do make eating easier and more pleasant.

plates: A medium-sized serving plate is adequate for all purposes.

bowls: Shallow soup bowls are not appropriate. Smallish, deep bowls measuring about 4½ inches across the

HOME COOKING

mouth and 2½–3 inches deep, with tapering sides and a rounded bottom are ideal. Whatever you have in the house that comes close to these dimensions is good. If rice is served, two such bowls are necessary—one for rice, and one for soup.

soup spoons: Chinese porcelain soup spoons are best, though any soup spoons will do. Chinese soup spoons are inexpensive, do not get hot, and can be used with Western food (stews and thick soups), if you like.

teacups: If you serve Chinese tea, a Western, handled teacup influences the flavor—why, I don't know. Chinese tea tastes infinitely better in small, handleless teacups. If they are elegant enough, Chinese teacups might be used to serve liqueurs, but actually I know of no better use for them than for Chinese tea.

chopsticks: If chopsticks are provided at a meal, a small chopstick rest is handy, but not essential. Plastic chopsticks, though required by law for restaurants in some cities, provide more problems in picking up slippery food than they are worth. Bamboo chopsticks are best; Japanese disposable chopsticks, though not elegant, are very convenient and easy to use.

Menu

With a cooking tradition as long as China's there is bound to be a great store of tradition and esoteric ideas about combinations of dishes and what constitutes a good menu. Yet new Chinese dishes are constantly being invented. The best principle to go by in making the menu for a Chinese meal is to do what you like. A good balance of fish, meat, and vegetables is the first and main criterion. Texture and color are later luxuries.

Usually a cook figures on the same number of dishes as there are diners, plus one soup, plus one sweet, if desired. For larger parties (over 8 diners), this calculation may get a little more complicated—a larger number of dishes than the number of diners might be best, depending on the richness of the food, the occasion, etc. Rich dishes of course go farther than blander foods, and can feed more with smaller quantities.

The number of servings for Chinese style dinners listed for each recipe is flexible, and depends on the total number of dishes served. To eat a little bit of many dishes is, of course, festive, and making Chinese food is a delight for the cook, whether dishes are served as main courses Western style or are created into elaborate Chinese banquets.

When eating rice, remember the farmers in the fields.

吃飯勿忘種田人

POULTRY

Jellied Chicken 鷄 凍
COLOR: PAGE 14

½ spring chicken
3 slices fresh ginger
½ stalk leek
1 stick agar-agar or 2–3 envelopes gelatin
3 cups chicken stock
½ tsp. salt
1 Tbsp. dry sherry
4 snow peas, washed, strung, and parboiled
5 slices carrot, cut in flower shapes and parboiled

Simmer chicken with ginger and leek in water to cover until tender. Remove from broth, then bone and slice. Reserve broth. Wash agar-agar, soak in water until soft, drain, and squeeze out water. Bring 3 cups stock to boil, add agar-agar, and boil until dissolved. Add salt and sherry (to taste), and set aside until lukewarm. Take care that the mixture does not set. Oil a gelatin mold or bowl with vegetable oil or shortening (do not use butter), and attractively arrange sliced chicken, snow peas, and carrots on the bottom and sides of mold. Carefully pour stock mixture into mold, and refrigerate until set. To loosen, immerse mold in boiling water briefly, put plate on top, and invert. Serves 3 as an aspic course. Serves 4–7 Chinese style.

Skewered Chicken Livers 炸鶏肝
COLOR: PAGE 14

12 chicken livers (livers of 6 chickens, lobes separated), cleaned
MARINADE
  1 tsp. ginger juice
  1 Tbsp. chopped leek
  1 Tbsp. soy sauce
  2 Tbsp. dry sherry
3 slices bacon, cut in fourths
Oil for deep frying
4 skewers

Mix marinade and marinate livers for 10 minutes, then drain and pat dry. Thread three livers and three bacon pieces alternately on each skewer. Heat oil to low (330°), and deep fry skewered livers until crisp. Serve hot or at room temperature as an hors d'oeuvre. Serves 4.

Note: Canned water chestnuts or fresh mushrooms may also be skewered and deep fried with the livers. Take care when deep frying livers because oil will spatter.

Chopped Chicken with Lettuce 炒鶏鬆
COLOR: PAGE 15

½ lb. boned chicken meat, diced
½ tsp. salt
Dash pepper
1 tsp. dry sherry
3 Tbsps. oil
2 Tbsps. oil
¼ cup canned water chestnuts or bamboo shoots, diced
¼ cup dried Chinese mushrooms, soaked in lukewarm water until tender, stemmed, and diced
¼ cup green peas, parboiled
SEASONINGS
  ½ tsp. salt
  ½ tsp. sugar
  1 Tbsp. dry sherry
  1 Tbsp. oyster sauce
  Dash pepper
1 head lettuce (romaine), leaves washed and separated

Mix chicken with salt, pepper and dry sherry, and let stand 5 minutes. Heat 3 Tbsps. oil, and stir-fry chicken on high heat until color changes. Set aside. Heat 2 Tbsps. oil, and stir-fry water chestnut, mushroom, and green peas on high heat 2 minutes. Add chicken and seasonings, and stir-fry 2 minutes. Place in serving bowl. Fill each lettuce leaf with one tablespoon of chicken mixture, and roll it up to eat. If desired, Chinese black bean paste or hoisin sauce may be used as

condiments. Serves 4 as a main course. Serves 6–8 Chinese style.

Duck with Chinese Cabbage 紅燒鴨
COLOR: PAGE 15

1 3-lb. duck, washed and patted dry
1 Tbsp. peppercorns, toasted and ground
1 Tbsp. salt
4 Tbsps. dry sherry
1 Tbsp. soy sauce
Oil for deep frying
1 stalk leek, cut in 2-in. lengths
2 slices fresh ginger
½ cup soy sauce
1 Tbsp. sugar
½ head Chinese cabbage
2 Tbsps. diced carrot
2 Tbsps. diced Chinese mushrooms
2 Tbsps. diced ham
2 Tbsps. green peas
1½ or 2 tsps. cornstarch mixed with 1 Tbsp. water

Rub cavity and skin of duck with freshly ground pepper and salt, then rub with sherry and soy sauce. Heat oil (360°), and deep fry duck until golden brown. Remove to deep pot, add leek, ginger, soy sauce, sugar, and water to cover, cover pot, and bring to boil on high heat. Reduce heat to low, and simmer about 2–2½ hours or until duck is tender. Remove to serving plate. Keep warm. Add vegetables and ham to remaining broth and cook on medium heat until tender. Add cornstarch mixture, stirring constantly until thickened. Pour the mixture over duck. Serve hot. Serves 4 as a main course. Serves 6–10 Chinese style.

Chicken Breast with Pineapple 鶏脯菠菜
COLOR: PAGE 16

½ lb. chicken breast, boned and cut in 2-in. squares
½ tsp. salt
1 tsp. cornstarch
3 Tbsps. oil
1 green pepper, cut in 2-in. squares
½ medium carrot, sliced and parboiled
SEASONINGS
   1 Tbsp. dry sherry
   1 tsp. salt
   ½ tsp. sugar
2 slices pineapple, cut in 2-in. wedges

Dredge chicken with salt and cornstarch. Heat oil, stir-fry chicken until white, and add green pepper, carrot, and seasonings. Stir-fry 2 minutes. Add pineapple, stir briefly, and serve hot. Serves 2 as a main course. Serves 4 Chinese style.

Braised Chicken with Black Bean Sauce 豆豉鶏

COLOR: PAGE 16

1 2-lb. spring chicken, washed, patted dry, and cut in 1½-in. pieces (with bone)
5 Tbsps. oil
1 stalk leek, finely chopped
3 slices fresh ginger
1 clove garlic, crushed
1 Tbsp. fermented black beans
SEASONINGS
    1 Tbsp. soy sauce
    1 tsp. sugar
    2 Tbsps. dry sherry
    ½ tsp. salt
1½ cups water
2 tsps. cornstarch mixed with ½ cup water

Heat oil, and briefly stir-fry leek, ginger, garlic, and fermented black beans. Add chicken, and stir-fry until brown. Add seasonings, stir, and add 1½ cups water. Cover, and simmer 30 minutes or until chicken is tender. Add cornstarch mixture, and stir constantly until well blended (3 minutes). Serve hot. Serves 3 as a main course. Serves 6–8 Chinese style.

Braised Duck with Onions 洋葱鴨

COLOR: PAGE 17

1 3-lb. duck
1 Tbsp. salt
1 Tbsp. soy sauce
3 Tbsps. oil
10 small onions
Oil for deep frying
SEASONINGS
    2 stalks leek, cut in 2-in. lengths
    2 slices fresh ginger
    3 Tbsps. soy sauce
    2 tsps. salt
    2 Tbsps. dry sherry
    2 Tbsps. sugar
    1 tsp. pepper
1 Tbsp. cornstarch mixed with ½ cup water

Wash duck, then rub cavity and skin with 1 Tbsp. salt. Wash again. Place duck in large saucepan, add water to cover, bring to boil, and cook briefly until the duck swells. Remove, wipe dry, and rub with 1 Tbsp. soy sauce. Discard boiling water. Heat 3 Tbsps. oil, and sauté onions over medium heat until light brown. Set aside. Heat oil (360°), and deep fry duck until golden brown. Remove to stewing pot. Cover with water. Add all seasonings, cover, bring to boil, and simmer one hour. Add sautéed onions, and continue simmering until duck is tender. Remove duck and onions from broth to a platter. Reserve broth. Add cornstarch mixture to broth, bring to boil, and stir briskly until thickened. Pour over duck on platter and garnish with parsley. Serve hot. Serves 4 as a main course. Serves 6–10 Chinese style.

Fried Duck
香酥鴨

COLOR: PAGE 18

1 3-lb. duck
2 Tbsps. whole peppercorns, toasted and ground
2 Tbsps. salt
2 Tbsps. dry sherry
3 stalks leek, cut in 3-in. lengths
3 slices fresh ginger
3 Tbsps. soy sauce
½ cup flour
Oil for deep frying
Tomato
Pineapple slices
Parsley

Mix freshly ground pepper and salt. Wash duck, and pat dry. Rub cavity and skin first with sherry and then with pepper-salt mixture. Place leek and ginger slices in cavity. Let stand 2-hours. Steam duck 2 hours or until tender. Cool. Rub with soy sauce, and coat with flour. Heat oil (360°), and deep fry duck until golden brown. Cut in 1 × 2-in. pieces. Arrange duck on platter, and garnish with tomato, pineapple and parsley. Serve with Chinese bread (see page 116) and dips of pepper-salt and ketchup. Serves 4 as a main course. Serves 6–10 Chinese style.

Lemon Chicken   檸檬鷄
COLOR: PAGE 19

1 1½-lb. spring chicken, cut in 2-in. pieces (with bone)
½ tsp. salt
5 Tbsps. oil
1 stalk leek, cut in 1-in. lengths
6 slices fresh ginger
1 lemon, sliced
SEASONINGS
  4 Tbsps. dry sherry
  6 Tbsps. soy sauce
  6 Tbsps. sugar
2 tsps. cornstarch mixed with 2 Tbsps. water

Sprinkle chicken with salt, and let stand 20 minutes. Heat oil, and stir-fry chicken, leek, and ginger until coated with oil. Add water to cover, then add lemon and seasonings, cover, and simmer 30 minutes. Add cornstarch mixture, and stir until thickened. Remove to serving plate, decorate with lemon slices, and serve hot. Serves 3 as a main course. Serves 4–8 Chinese style.

Note: If a boiling chicken is used, the simmering period should be longer, and the water should be increased.

Chicken with Chestnuts   栗子鷄
COLOR: PAGE 22

½ spring chicken, cut in bite-sized pieces (with bone)
4 Tbsps. oil
1 stalk leek, cut in 2-in. lengths
4 slices fresh ginger
½ tsp. salt
4 Tbsps. soy sauce
1 Tbsps. dry sherry
1 cup water
6 chestnuts, shelled and inner skin removed
½ Tbsp. sugar
1 Tbsp. finely chopped parsley

Heat oil, add leek, ginger and chicken, and stir-fry until chicken is golden. Add salt, soy sauce, sherry and water. Bring to boil, cover pan, reduce heat to low, and simmer 20 minutes. Add chestnuts and sugar, and simmer another 15 minutes or until tender. Remove to serving plate, and sprinkle with parsley. Serve hot. Serves 2 as a main course. Serves 4–6 Chinese style.

If the mouth is too full, chewing is difficult.

貧多嚼不爛

Fried Chicken (whole) 脆皮雞
COLOR: PAGE 23

1 2-lb. spring chicken
MARINADE
    1½ Tbsps. salt
    Dash pepper
    1 clove star anise, crushed
    1 stalk leek, cut in 1-in. lengths
    1 Tbsp. dry sherry
    2 tsps. grated fresh ginger
SEASONINGS
    1 Tbsps. dry sherry
    2 Tbsps. white vinegar
    1 Tbsp. honey or corn syrup
Oil for deep frying

Rub chicken cavity and skin with marinade, and let stand about 1 hour. Bring ample amount of water to boil, add chicken, and simmer 20 minutes. Remove, cool, and carefully pat dry inside and out. Rub with seasonings, and let stand until dry. Heat oil (360°), and deep fry chicken until skin becomes crisp. Cut in bite-sized pieces, and serve hot or cold with pepper-salt and ketchup as dips. Serves 3 as a main course. Serves 6–8 Chinese style.

Drunk Chicken 醉雞
COLOR: PAGE 24

1 2-lb. spring chicken
1½ Tbsps. salt
1 Tbsp. ginger juice
2 stalks leek, cut in 2-in. lengths
½ tsp. powdered star anise
2 cups dry sherry
½ cup finely shredded leek

Wash chicken, pat dry, and rub cavity and skin with salt and ginger juice. Place leek and powdered star anise in cavity. Let stand 2 hours; pour 1 cup sherry over chicken, and let stand 2 hours more, turning at least four times. Put chicken in bowl, and steam 30 minutes. Remove from heat, reserving broth remaining in bowl. Cool, and cut in quarters. Put chicken back in the bowl with broth. Add the remaining cup sherry. Cover bowl, and let stand 4 hours or overnight in refrigerator. Cut each quarter in bite-sized pieces. Arrange on plate and garnish with finely shredded leek. Serve cold. Serves 3 as a main course. Serves 6–10 Chinese style.

Note: This chicken may be kept in refrigerator for one week. A boiler hen has more flavor than a spring chicken, but must be steamed 1½ hours.

Steamed Chicken with Ham   鶏片蒸火腿
COLOR: PAGE 25

½ spring chicken
½ tsp. salt
½ lb. ham, sliced
1 Tbsp. dry sherry
½ cup sugar
1 cup broth from steamed chicken
2 tsps. cornstarch mixed with 2 Tbsps. water
4 canned loquats

Rub chicken with salt, place in bowl, and let stand 20 minutes. Place bowl with chicken in steamer, and steam 20 minutes. Cool, and slice chicken. Reserve broth remaining in bowl. Marinate ham in sherry and sugar 10 minutes, place on a deep plate, and steam 15 minutes. Arrange on a platter with chicken slices. Heat 1 cup broth from the steamed chicken, add cornstarch mixture, and simmer, stirring constantly, until thickened. Pour sauce over chicken and ham. Garnish with loquats. Serve hot. Serves 2 as a main course. Serves 2–4 Chinese style.

Sautéed Chicken Livers with Celery   鶏肝炒芹菜
COLOR: PAGE 28

6 chicken livers (livers of 3 chickens, lobes separated), cleaned, thickly sliced, and parboiled
½ tsp. ginger juice
1 tsp. dry sherry
1 tsp. cornstarch
2 Tbsps. oil
6 oz. fresh scallops, thickly sliced lengthwise
2 Tbsps. oil
1 stalk leek, cut in 2-in. lengths
3 slices fresh ginger
1 stalk celery, washed and cut in ½ × 1½-in. pieces
SEASONINGS
    1 Tbsp. dry sherry
    2 Tbsps. soy sauce
    1 tsp. sugar

Mix parboiled liver with ginger juice, sherry and cornstarch. Heat 2 Tbsps. oil, and stir-fry liver and scallops over high heat until color changes. Remove from pan. Heat 2 Tbsps. oil, add leek, ginger, and celery, and stir-fry briefly. Add liver, scallops, and seasonings, and stir-fry a few minutes. Serve hot. Serves 2 as a main course. Serves 4–6 Chinese style.

Fried Chicken (pieces) 炸鷄塊
COLOR: PAGE 28

1 2-lb. spring chicken, cut in bite-sized pieces (with bone)
MARINADE
    1 stalk leek, finely chopped
    1 Tbsp. dry sherry
    Dash pepper
BATTER
    1 egg, lightly beaten
    6 Tbsps. flour
Oil for deep frying

Mix marinade, and marinate chicken 10 minutes. Mix batter ingredients. Heat oil (360°). Coat chicken pieces with batter, and deep fry until crisp. Serve hot. Serves 3 as a main course. Serves 6–8 Chinese style.

White Chicken 白鷄
COLOR: PAGE 29

1 spring chicken
1 stalk leek, cut in 1-in. lengths
3 slices fresh ginger
soy sauce
sesame oil

Add chicken, leek, and ginger to 10 cups boiling water. Bring to boil, reduce heat, and simmer 30 minutes. Remove from heat; let chicken cool in the pan. When cool, rinse chicken under cold running water to make skin shiny and firm. Slice before serving. Sprinkle with soy sauce and sesame oil. Serves 3 as a main course. Serves 6–8 Chinese style.

Longevity Chicken 枸子准山鷄
COLOR: PAGE 31

1 boiling chicken
⅛ lb. *kou tzu* seeds
⅛ lb. *chün shan* wafers
2 slices fresh ginger
½ stalk leek
2 tsps. salt

Place chicken in deep saucepan, cover with water, and add all ingredients. Bring to boil, reduce heat, cover, and simmer 2 hours or until seeds and chicken are tender. Serve hot. Serves 3–4 as a main course. Serves 6–10 Chinese style.

Note: This succulent soup is good for the eyes and blood. The herbs, *kou tzu* (枸子) and *chün shan* (准山) in Chinese, should be readily available at Chinese medicine or herb shops. I have tried to find out the botanical identity of these two herbs, but with limited success. *Kou tzu* is most probably the seeds of *Lycium chinense*, the leaves and roots of which also have medicinal uses. The white *chün shan* wafers are also called *fu p'ien* (馥片) and *ling yün* (靈雲), and are probably slices of a root or tuber. These names seem to refer to the object and not the plant, and no book consulted had the botanical information. Nevertheless, both are common Chinese herbs, and the appropriate specialty shops should stock them.

Chicken with Walnuts 炒核桃鷄丁
COLOR: PAGE 33

½ lb. boned chicken meat, cut in 1 × ½-in. pieces
½ tsp. salt
1 tsp. dry sherry
1 tsp. cornstarch
3 Tbsps. oil
Oil for deep frying
½ cup walnuts, blanched by soaking in boiling water 15 minutes, drained, and patted dry
1 Tbsp. oil
2 green peppers, cut in 1-in. squares
SEASONINGS
    1 tsp. sugar
    1 tsp. dry sherry
    1 Tbsp. soy sauce
    ½ tsp. vinegar
1 tsp. cornstarch mixed with 1 Tbsp. water

Mix chicken with salt, sherry and cornstarch. Heat 3 Tbsps. oil, and stir-fry chicken over high heat until color changes. Set aside. Heat oil to medium (340°), and deep fry walnuts until slightly browned. Heat 1 Tbsp. oil, and stir-fry green pepper over high heat 2–3 minutes, add fried chicken, walnuts and seasonings, and stir-fry briefly. Add cornstarch mixture, and stir until thickened. Serve hot. Serves 2 as a main course. Serves 4 Chinese style.

Sweet and Sour Fish 糖醋魚
COLOR: PAGE 13

½ lb. white meat fish fillet, cut in ½ × 2-in. strips
MARINADE
    ½ Tbsp. dry sherry
    1 Tbsp. soy sauce
    1 Tbsp. flour
    1 Tbsp. cornstarch
Oil for deep frying
3 Tbsps. oil
1 medium onion, cut in ½-in. wedges and layers separated
1 green pepper, seeded and cut in ½ × 2-in. strips
1 small carrot, cut in ½ × 2-in. strips and parboiled
SAUCE
    ⅓ cup sugar
    ⅓ cup ketchup
    3 Tbsps. vinegar
    2 Tbsps. dry sherry
    ½ cup water
1 Tbsp. cornstarch mixed with 1 Tbsp. water
1 pineapple slice, cut in 6 pieces
6 cherries

Mix fish well with marinade. Heat oil to medium (340°). Separate fish pieces, and deep fry until crisp. Drain on absorbent paper. Heat 3 Tbsps. oil, and stir-fry onion, green pepper, and carrot over high heat 1 minute. Add sauce ingredients, and bring to boil, stirring briskly. Add cornstarch mixture, and stir until thickened. Add

FISH

fried fish, and stir briefly. Arrange on serving plate with pineapple and cherries, and serve hot. Serves 2 as a main course. Serves 4–6 Chinese style.

Steamed Salmon with Eggs 蛋蒸魚
COLOR: PAGE 16

4 salmon fillets
1 tsp. salt
1 Tbsp. dry sherry
4 eggs
Pinch salt

Place sliced salmon on a plate, and sprinkle with 1 tsp. salt and sherry. Break eggs, place on top of salmon, and sprinkle with salt to taste. Steam 15 minutes. Serves 2 as a main course. Serves 4–6 Chinese style.

Note: Use salted duck eggs in place of chicken eggs, if available.

Steamed Fish 清蒸魚
COLOR: PAGE 21

1 1½-lb. white meat fish, scaled, head and tail left intact
1 Tbsp. cornstarch
4 slices fresh ginger
½ stalk leek, sliced diagonally in 8 pieces
8 2 × 1-in. slices ham
8 2 × 1-in. slices canned bamboo shoots
2 large dried Chinese mushrooms, soaked in lukewarm water until tender, each cut in 4 slices
1 Tbsp. dry sherry
2 stalks spinach, washed and stems removed
SAUCE
    1 tsp. ginger juice
    1 Tbsp. sugar
    2 Tbsps. vinegar
    1 Tbsp. soy sauce

Cut 8 diagonal cuts almost touching the bone on each side of fish. Sprinkle fish with cornstarch on both sides. Place sliced ginger, leek, ham, bamboo shoot, and mushroom in diagonal cuts of fish. Place fish on plate, sprinkle with sherry, and put in steamer. Steam 20 minutes with spinach leaves. Remove from steamer. Mix sauce ingredients well. Pour over steamed fish before serving. Serve hot. Serves 2 as a main course. Serves 4–6 Chinese style.

Note: The oven may be used for steaming a large fish.

Fill a deep roasting pan with 1 inch water. Place fish in a deep platter with edges well above water level; cover platter with aluminium foil securely. Place in roasting pan, and steam in high oven (470°) for 15 minutes.

Braised Fish with Beancurd 砂鍋魚燉豆腐

COLOR: PAGE 22

1 1-lb. white meat fish, cleaned, filleted or left whole
2 Tbsps. dry sherry
2 Tbsps. soy sauce
3 Tbsps. flour
4 Tbsps. oil
1 stalk leek, cut in 2-in. lengths
2 slices ham, quartered
3 dried Chinese mushrooms, soaked in lukewarm water until tender, stemmed, and quartered

SEASONINGS
    1 Tbsp. dry sherry
    5 Tbsps. soy sauce
    1 Tbsp. sugar

¾ cup water
1 cake beancurd, cut in 1-in. cubes
¼ package transparent vermicelli, soaked in lukewarm water until tender

Sprinkle fish with sherry, soy sauce, and flour. Heat oil, and lightly brown fish on both sides. Add leek, ham, mushrooms, seasonings, and water. Bring to boil quickly over high heat. Reduce heat to low, and simmer 20 minutes. Add beancurd and vermicelli, and simmer another 10 minutes. Serve hot in casserole or deep serving dish. Serves 2 as a main course. Serves 4–6 Chinese style.

Spiced Fish Slices 燻魚
COLOR: PAGE 29

6 fish fillets (any fish may be used)
MARINADE
    1 tsp. salt
    2 tsps. dry sherry
    Dash pepper
    1 stalk leek, cut in ½-in. lengths
    3 slices fresh ginger
Oil for deep frying
SAUCE
    1 clove star anise
    1 tsp. powdered cinnamon
    1 Tbsp. grated orange peel
    1 Tbsp. soy sauce
    2 Tbsps. sugar
    2 Tbsps. dry sherry
    ½ cup water

Mix marinade, and marinate fish overnight. Heat oil (360°), and deep fry fish until golden brown. Place sauce ingredients in heavy pan, bring to boil, add fish, and simmer until liquid almost disappears (about 15 minutes). Serve at room temperature. Serves 3 as a main course. Serves 6 Chinese style.

Note: The flavor of the fish will be enhanced if cross-section slices including the bones are used rather than boned fillets.

SHELLFISH

Cold Lobster 龍蝦沙律
COLOR: PAGE 13

1 lobster, washed in cold water
SEASONINGS
- *1 tsp. vinegar*
- *1 tsp. sesame oil*
- *½ tsp. salt*
- *1 Tbsp. dry sherry*

Place lobster on damp cheesecloth in steamer, and steam over high heat 20 minutes. Remove, and cool. Remove meat from shell, and slice. Arrange on plate. Mix seasonings, and pour over lobster before eating. Serve at room temperature. Serves 2 as a main course. Serves 4–6 Chinese style.

Note: If desired, sliced cucumber may be arranged under the lobster meat. If the shell is to be used for a decorative arrangement, first tie the feelers back over the lobster's head with string, and skewer the entire body with a long chopstick or barbecue skewer to prevent curling while steaming.

Spicy Shrimp 塩焗蝦
COLOR: PAGE 14

2 Tbsps. oil
1 lb. shrimp, washed in salted water, shells left intact
SEASONINGS
    ½ tsp. powdered red chili pepper
    1 tsp. powdered ginger
    2 Tbsps. onion powder
    ½ tsp. powdered star anise
    1 tsp. sesame oil
    1 tsp. salt
    ½ tsp. sugar
    1 Tbsp. dry sherry
2 Tbsps. water

Heat oil, and stir-fry shrimp on high heat until color changes. Add all seasonings, and stir-fry briefly. Add water, cover, and simmer until all the water is gone. Serve hot or at room temperature. Serves 2 as a main course. Serves 4–6 Chinese style.

Shrimp with Celery 芹菜炒蝦仁
COLOR: PAGE 18

1 cup shrimp, shelled and deveined
SEASONINGS A
    ½ tsp. salt
    Dash pepper
    ½ tsp. dry sherry
    2 tsps. egg white
    ½ tsp. cornstarch
Oil for deep frying
1 Tbsp. oil
1 clove garlic, crushed
½ medium carrot, sliced and parboiled
1 stalk celery, sliced diagonally
SEASONINGS B
    ½ tsp. salt
    ½ tsp. sugar
    1 tsp. dry sherry
1 Tbsp. green peas
½ tsp. cornstarch mixed with 3 Tbsps. water

Wash shrimp in salted water, drain, and pat dry. Add seasonings A, and mix well. Heat oil to medium (340°), and deep fry shrimp until just pink. Remove. Heat 1 Tbsp. oil, sauté garlic on low heat until golden, discard garlic, add carrot and celery, and stir-fry 2 minutes. Add shrimp, seasonings B, and green peas, stir-fry about 1 minute on high heat, and add cornstarch mixture, stirring briskly until thickened. Serve hot. Serves 2 as a main course. Serves 4–6 Chinese style.

Two-Color Shrimp Balls 鴛鴦蝦球
COLOR: PAGE 21

1 lb. shrimp, shelled, deveined, and finely chopped
½ tsp. salt
1 egg white
1 Tbsp. cornstarch
1 Tbsp. dry sherry
1 tsp. oil
Dash pepper
2 Tbsps. ketchup
Oil for deep frying

Combine shrimp with salt, egg white, cornstarch, sherry, oil, and pepper. Divide mixture into halves, and mix one half with 2 Tbsps. ketchup. Wet hands, and make walnut-sized balls with approximately 1 heaped Tbsp. of mixture. Heat oil (360°). Drop the shrimp balls into the hot oil a few at a time, taking care that they do not stick together. When the balls have floated to the top and become crisp (about 2 minutes), remove and drain on absorbent paper. Serve hot with ketchup and pepper-salt as dips. Serves 4–6 as an hors d'oeuvre or Chinese style.

Sweet and Sour Prawns 糖醋大蝦
COLOR: PAGE 22

10 prawns, washed, slit deeply down back, and deveined
  (without removing shell)
Oil for deep frying
SEASONINGS
  5 Tbsps. sugar
  2 Tbsps. dry sherry
  1 tsp. salt
  Dash pepper
  3 Tbsps. vinegar
2 tsps. cornstarch mixed with ½ cup water

Heat oil (360°), and deep fry prawns until just pink. Drain on absorbent paper. Mix seasonings, place in saucepan, and bring to boil. Add cornstarch mixture, and stir until thickened. Add shrimp, mix briefly, and remove to serving plate. Serve hot. Serves 2–3 as a main course. Serves 6–10 Chinese style.

Note: If desired, prawns may be shelled.

When the eldest sister makes shoes, the second sister makes shoes.

大姐作鞋二姐照樣

Fried Shrimp 清炸蝦仁
COLOR: PAGE 28

1½ lbs. medium shrimp, shelled and deveined
1 Tbsp. salt
COATING
    1 tsp. salt
    ½ egg white
    1 Tbsp. cornstarch
Oil for deep frying
1 Tbsp. oil
½ cup green peas
SEASONINGS
    ½ tsp. salt
    Dash pepper
    2 tsps. dry sherry
    ½ tsp. sesame oil

Rub shrimp with 1 Tbsp. salt, wash with water two or three times, and pat dry. Mix shrimp with coating mixture. Heat oil (360°), deep fry shrimp until just pink, remove, and drain. Heat 1 Tbsp. oil, stir-fry green peas on high heat, and add fried shrimp and seasonings. Stir-fry 1 minute. Serve hot. Serves 2–3 as a main course. Serves 6–8 Chinese style.

Sesame Shrimp Toast 芝麻蝦扡
COLOR: PAGE 31

1 lb. shrimp, shelled, deveined, and finely chopped
4 Tbsps. finely chopped pork fat
SEASONINGS
    ½ egg white
    1 Tbsp. chopped parsley
    1 Tbsp. chopped leek or onion
    1 tsp. salt
    1 tsp. sugar
    1 tsp. dry sherry
    1 Tbsp. cornstarch
    Dash pepper
6 slices white bread, crust trimmed
4 oz. sesame seeds (white or black)
Oil for deep frying

Mix shrimp, pork fat, and seasonings thoroughly until mixture holds together. Cover, and refrigerate until chilled (this step may be done one day in advance). Spread chilled shrimp mixture on bread slices. Sprinkle with sesame seeds. Heat oil to medium (340°), and place bread slices in hot oil one by one, shrimp side down. When shrimp side is lightly browned, turn over, and fry until the same color. Remove, and drain on absorbent paper. Cut either in bite-sized squares or in finger strips. Serve hot or at room temperature on platter with parsley for garnish. Serves 10–18 as an hors d'oeuvre or Chinese style.

Fried Oysters with Asparagus
蠔炸生酥・龍鬚菜

COLOR: PAGE 20

½ lb. oysters
1 Tbsp. salt
3 Tbsps. cornstarch
Pinch salt
Dash pepper
¼ cup flour
1 egg, beaten lightly
½ cup bread crumbs
Oil for deep frying
½ lb. asparagus, hard stems removed, parboiled in salted water, and drained
2 Tbsps. oil
1 tsp. salt
½ tsp. sugar

Sprinkle oysters with 1 Tbsp. salt and 3 Tbsps. cornstarch, stir well, and rinse under running water until clean. Place in boiling water 2 seconds, remove, drain, and pat dry. Sprinkle with salt and pepper. Coat with flour, dip in beaten egg, and roll in bread crumbs. Heat oil (360°), and deep fry oysters until golden brown. Drain. Heat 2 Tbsps. oil, stir-fry asparagus on high heat until coated with oil, season with salt and pepper, and stir-fry about 1 minute longer. Arrange fried oysters and asparagus on serving plate, and serve hot with pepper-salt as dip. Serves 2 as a main course. Serves 4-6 Chinese style.

Scallops and Chicken Livers with Celery
炒雞肝芹菜

COLOR: PAGE 25

2 Tbsps. oil
2 stalks celery, cut in ½-in. slices
5 Tbsps. oil
1 lb. large scallops, cut in ¼-in. slices
8 chicken livers (livers of 4 chickens, lobes separated), cleaned

SEASONINGS
    2 Tbsps. dry sherry
    1 tsp. ginger juice
    Dash pepper
    ½ tsp. salt
    1 Tbsp. soy sauce

Heat 2 Tbsps. oil. Stir-fry celery briefly to soften. Set aside. Heat 5 Tbsps. oil, stir-fry scallops and liver until tender. Add seasonings and celery, and stir-fry 2 minutes. Serve hot. Serves 2 as a main course. Serves 5-6 Chinese style.

Note: If small scallops are used, cut in half.

Fried Crab Claws

蟹 角

COLOR: PAGE 17

8 large crab claws
1 stalk leek, cut in 3-in. lengths
2 slices fresh ginger
1 lb. shrimp, washed, shelled, deveined, and patted dry
1 tsp. salt
Dash pepper
½ tsp. ginger juice or a dash of powdered ginger
1 Tbsp. dry sherry
1 egg white
½ Tbsp. cornstarch
Oil for deep frying
Cornstarch

Clean crab claws, and steam with leek and ginger about 15 minutes until color is bright red. Remove, and cool. Crack, remove shell carefully (including movable pincer), leaving large meaty part attached to one pincer (see color photo, p. 17), and let stand until thoroughly dry. Crush shrimp under the side of broad knife or cleaver, chop finely, and place in bowl. Add salt, pepper to taste, ginger juice, sherry, egg white, and ½ Tbsp. cornstarch, then mix thoroughly until shrimp mixture holds together. Generously coat crab claws with shrimp mixture, then coat with cornstarch. Heat oil (360°), and place crab claws in hot oil one by one. Turn slowly with chopsticks or slotted spoon while deep frying. When golden brown and crisp, remove from oil, and drain on absorbent paper. Arrange on platter, and garnish with parsley. Serve with pepper-salt and ketchup as dips. Serves 2–3 as a main course. Serves 4–8 as an hors d'oeuvre or Chinese style.

Note: Lemon slices may be added as a garnish.

Crab with Black Bean Sauce 豆豉蟹
COLOR: PAGE 26

1 large softshell crab, washed, cleaned, and cut in 3-in. pieces (with shell)
½ tsp. grated fresh ginger
½ tsp. grated garlic
Cornstarch
Oil for deep frying
3 Tbsps. oil
½ stalk leek, finely chopped
2 Tbsps. fermented black beans
SEASONINGS
    1 Tbsp. dry sherry
    2 Tbsps. soy sauce
    2 Tbsps. sugar
    ½ tsp. sesame oil
½ cup soup stock
1 tsp. cornstarch mixed with 2 Tbsps. water

Mix crab with ginger and garlic. Coat lightly with cornstarch. Heat oil (360°), and deep fry crab briefly until color changes. Heat 3 Tbsps. oil, and stir-fry leek and fermented black beans for 2 minutes. Add crab, seasonings and soup stock, bring to boil, and simmer 10 minutes. Add cornstarch mixture, and stir until thickened. Serve hot. Serves 2 as a main course. Serves 4–6 Chinese style.

Jellyfish and Cucumber 海蜇皮拌黃瓜
COLOR: PAGE 19

2 cups shredded jellyfish
1 cup shredded cucumber
2 Tbsps. oil
½ cup shredded pork
SEASONINGS
    2 tsps. soy sauce
    1 tsp. salt
    Dash pepper
1 egg, beaten
SAUCE
    2 Tbsps. vinegar
    1 Tbsp. soy sauce
    2 tsps. sesame oil
    1 tsp. powdered mustard

Prepare jellyfish three days in advance (see page 45). Fold in pleats or layers, then cut across layers to shred. Spread on platter. Top with layer of shredded cucumber. Heat oil, stir-fry pork on high heat until just light brown, add seasonings, stir-fry 1 minute, remove, and cool. Place in center of cucumber. Heat a thin coating of oil in 9-inch skillet, and pour in half of beaten egg to make a thin crepe. Remove when firm, and shred. Repeat the same process with remaining egg. Spread around pork. Mix sauce, and pour over the dish just before serving. Serve at room temperature. Serves 2 as a main course. Serves 6–8 Chinese style.

Stir-Fried Cuttlefish

炒魷魚

COLOR: PAGE 20

1 lb. cuttlefish
MARINADE
    1 tsp. ginger juice
    ½ tsp. sugar
    ½ tsp. salt
    Dash pepper
    1 tsp. cornstarch
4 Tbsps. oil
1 clove garlic, crushed
1 green pepper, seeded and cut in 1-in. squares
4 slices carrot, parboiled
½ stalk leek, cut in ½-in. lengths
SEASONINGS
    1 Tbsp. dry sherry
    Pinch salt
    Dash pepper
1 tsp. cornstarch mixed with 2 Tbsps. water

Cut open cuttlefish and remove intestines and all the thin skin. Discard head and legs. Wash, and deeply score the outside surface in a crisscross pattern (see process photos, p. 52). Cut in 2-in. squares. Mix marinade, and marinate cuttlefish 10 minutes. Heat oil, brown garlic on medium heat, and discard. Add cuttlefish, green pepper, carrot, and leek, and stir-fry 2 minutes. Add sherry, salt, and pepper, and stir-fry 1 minute. Add cornstarch mixture, stirring constantly until thickened. Serve hot. Serves 2 as a main course. Serves 4–6 Chinese style.

Note: If cooking period is too long, the cuttlefish toughens. If desired, add 2 Tbsps. oyster sauce with seasonings.

BEEF

Ground Beef with Green Peas 牛內末炒青豆
COLOR: PAGE 14

½ lb. ground beef
1 egg white
1 tsp. cornstarch
4 Tbsps. oil
SEASONINGS
    1 Tbsp. dry sherry
    1 Tbsp. soy sauce
    ½ tsp. salt
    ½ tsp. sugar
1 cup green peas, parboiled

Mix ground beef well with egg white and cornstarch. Heat oil, and stir-fry ground beef until color changes. Add seasonings, and stir-fry 1 minute. Add green peas, mix well, and serve immediately. Serves 2 as a main course. Serves 4–6 Chinese style.

Chinese Beef Steak 中式牛排
COLOR: PAGE 25

4 minute steaks, quartered
1 clove garlic, grated
1 tsp. ginger juice
4 Tbsps. oil
2 Tbsps. dry sherry
2 Tbsps. soy sauce
½ tsp. cornstarch mixed with 2 Tbsps. water
2 cups shredded cabbage
Canned lichees (optional)
Canned cherries (optional)

Marinate beef with garlic and ginger juice 10 minutes. Heat oil, and stir-fry beef until brown. Add sherry and soy sauce, and stir-fry until it begins to smoke. Add cornstarch mixture, and stir until thickened. Serve hot over shredded cabbage. Decorate with lichees stuffed with cherries, if desired. Serves 2 as a main course. Serves 4-6 Chinese style.

Beef with Shredded Potatoes 煎牛肉上豆絲

½ lb. beef tenderloin, cut in 2 × 3-in. slices
MARINADE
    1 tsp. dry sherry
    1 tsp. soy sauce
    1 tsp. cornstarch
Oil for deep frying
2 medium potatoes, peeled, roughly grated, soaked in water 5 minutes, drained, and patted dry
3 Tbsps. oil
SEASONINGS
    1 Tbsp. dry sherry
    1 Tbsp. soy sauce
    ½ tsp. salt
    ½ tsp. sugar
1 Tbsp. cornstarch mixed with 3 Tbsps. water

Mix marinade ingredients, and marinate beef 15 minutes. Heat oil (360°), and add grated potato a little at a time. Stir to separate the potato shreds. Fry until crisp and golden, then remove, and drain on absorbent paper. Heat 3 Tbsps. oil, add beef, and stir-fry until color changes. Add seasonings, and stir-fry 1 minute. Add cornstarch mixture, and stir until thickened. Serve hot on top of fried, grated potatoes. Serves 2 as a main course. Serves 4-6 Chinese style.

Beef with Broccoli 牛肉炒芥蘭
COLOR: PAGE 26

½ lb. lean beef, cut in bite-sized slices
1 tsp. soy sauce
1 tsp. cornstarch
3 Tbsps. oil
3–4 slices fresh ginger
1 stalk broccoli, flowerets separated, stem skinned, thinly sliced diagonally, and parboiled
SEASONINGS
    1 tsp. salt
    ½ tsp. sugar
    2 tsps. soy sauce

Mix beef with soy sauce and cornstarch. Heat oil, add sliced ginger, and stir 3–4 times. Add beef, and stir-fry until color changes. Add broccoli and seasonings, and stir-fry 1 minute. Serve hot. Serves 2 as a main course. Serves 4–6 Chinese style.

Stir-Fried Beef with Snow Peas 牛肉炒青豆
COLOR: PAGE 28

½ lb. lean beef, very thinly sliced
MARINADE
    1 tsp. soy sauce
    1 Tbsp. dry sherry
    ½ tsp. salt
    Dash pepper
    2 tsps. cornstarch
½ cup oil
½ lb. snow peas, washed and stringed
9 carrot slices (cut in decorative shapes if desired)
⅓ tsp. salt
3 Tbsps. water
2 Tbsps. oil
SEASONINGS
    ½ tsp. sugar
    1 Tbsp. soy sauce
    1 tsp. ginger juice

Mix marinade ingredients, and marinate sliced beef 15 minutes. Heat ½ cup oil to medium (340°). Fry beef briefly until brown. Remove from oil, and set aside. Heat 1 Tbsp. oil, and stir-fry snow peas and carrot briefly. Add salt and water, cover, and cook on medium heat until liquid evaporates. Arrange on serving plate. Heat remaining 1 Tbsp. oil, and stir-fry fried beef with seasonings briefly. Remove to plate with snow peas. Serve hot. Serves 2 as a main course. Serves 4–6 Chinese style.

Anise Braised Beef

茴香牛肉

COLOR: PAGE 29

2 lbs. boneless beef shank
2 Tbsps. oil
1 stalk leek, cut in 3-in. lengths
3 Tbsps. dry sherry
4 slices fresh ginger
½ tsp. salt
4 Tbsps. soy sauce
1 clove star anise

Heat oil in Dutch oven, and brown beef on all sides. Add remaining ingredients and water to cover, bring to boil, and simmer 3 hours. Remove to bowl with broth. Cool, and then refrigerate until chilled. Cut beef in thin slices, and arrange on plate with parsley for garnish. Serves 2 as a main course. Serves 4-6 Chinese style.

*Quarreling makes a good marriage;
a quiet marriage does not last long.*

好夫妻打到頭，不打不罵不長久

PORK

Cold Cut Arrangement 冷拼盤
COLOR: PAGE 13

HAM

Any kind of boiled ham may be used. Slices should be approximately 1 × 2 inches.

TONGUE

Thoroughly clean 2 pork tongues (a beef tongue tip may be used). Simmer 20 minutes, remove skin, and simmer again with ½ stalk leek, 3 slices ginger, 1 Tbsp. soy sauce, and 1 Tbsp. dry sherry for 1 hour or until tender. Place tongue on side and thinly slice diagonally.

CHICKEN BREAST

Bone, skin, and shred breast of White Chicken (see p. 67). Boiled chicken breast may also be used.

BARBECUED PORK

See recipe, page 90. Slice diagonally.

ABALONE

Canned abalone can be thinly sliced and used as is, but the flavor is enhanced if it is steamed for 20 minutes with ½ stalk leek and 2–3 slices ginger, then cooled and sliced.

BRAISED MUSHROOMS

¼ lb. dried Chinese mushrooms, soaked in lukewarm water until tender, stemmed, and water squeezed out
2 Tbsps. oil

SEASONINGS
    2 Tbsps. soy sauce
    1 Tbsp. sugar
    1 Tbsp. sesame oil
½ cup water

Heat oil, add mushrooms, and stir-fry about 30 seconds. Add seasonings and water, and simmer until liquid evaporates. Cool and slice diagonally.

CUCUMBER

Rub one cucumber with salt, then wash. Cut in half lengthwise (quarters might be necessary for a large cucumber), and thinly slice diagonally.

EGG YOLK

Beat the yolks of 3 eggs with a pinch of salt just until well blended. Place in an oiled (do not use butter) porcelain butter dish or an appropriate heatproof container to allow an egg thickness of 1 inch. Steam using soup stock or water over medium heat for 15 minutes or until set. Cool and thinly slice.

Trying to make cold cuts into a design is a bit tricky at first. You may wish to make geometric patterns before trying more complex arrangements, in order to get the feel of how the different ingredients combine. Nonetheless, the falcon pictured on page 13 is a relatively easy goal. Once realism is mastered, you may with to try your luck at becoming a cold cut Picasso.

Arranging slices: pick up each slice with the left hand and slide knife under right edge, then arrange the slices one by one in the appropriate rows or arcs. Slide the knife under the entire row or arc of slices and place it as a unit in the design, then correct for shape if necessary. Work from the outside in or vice versa, as you prefer. The falcon was made from the wing tips in, but control of proportions might prove difficult at first with this order, and I recommend that you start with the body and work out to the wings. Serves 6–8.

Pork with Plums 酸梅蒸猪肉

COLOR: PAGE 16

1 lb. lean pork, cut in bite-sized slices
8 dried, preserved plums, slit once
1 tsp. cornstarch
1 tsp. dry sherry
1 tsp. soy sauce
1 tsp. salt
1 tsp. sugar
2 Tbsps. oil

Mix all ingredients except oil, and let stand 10 minutes. Place in deep plate or shallow bowl, and sprinkle with oil. Place in steamer, and steam 15 minutes. Serve hot. Serves 2 as a main course. Serves 4–6 Chinese style.

Note: Two tsps. fermented black beans may be added to the pork mixture to enhance flavor. Beef may be substituted for pork. Also, 2 Tbsps. rice flour or fast-cooking farina will enrich this dish.

1. tongue
2. abalone
3. cucumber
4. mushroom
5. egg yolk
6. ham
7. chicken breast
8. barbecued pork
9. pimento

Fried Pork with Pickles 肉絲炒雪菜
COLOR: PAGE 17

½ lb. lean pork, shredded
½ tsp. cornstarch mixed with ½ tsp. salt
2 Tbsps. oil
1 cup or ½ lb. shredded Chinese salty pickles (Szechwan pickles or Chinese pickled cabbage)
2 Tbsps. oil
2 Tbsps. chopped leek
1 Tbsp. sugar

Dredge pork with cornstarch-salt mixture, and let stand 10 minutes. Heat 2 Tbsps. oil, stir-fry pickles on high heat 1 minute, and remove. Heat another 2 Tbsps. oil, stir-fry leek and pork on high heat until color changes, add pickles and sugar, and stir-fry 1 minute. Serve hot or cold. Serves 2 as a main course. Serves 4–8 Chinese style.

Barbecued Spareribs 烤大排骨
COLOR: PAGE 23

2½ lbs. spareribs, uncut (rib rack)
MARINADE
    3 Tbsps. dry sherry
    4 Tbsps. soy sauce
    2 tsps. grated garlic
1 pineapple, peeled and quartered lengthwise
2 Tbsps. corn syrup

Line a roasting pan with aluminum foil. Place the rib rack on foil, rub with marinade, and pour the remaining marinade over it. Let stand 2–3 hours. Heat oven to 350°. Roast 25 minutes. Place 2 pineapple quarters beside ribs. Brush spareribs with syrup two or three times while roasting another 15 minutes or until well done. Separate ribs before serving. Serve hot. Serves 2 as a main course. Serves 6–8 Chinese style.

Braised Spareribs 醬油烤排骨
COLOR: PAGE 24

1½ lbs. spareribs, cut in 2- or 3-in. pieces
1 tsp. salt
3 Tbsps. oil
2 Tbsps. soy sauce
1 Tbsp. dry sherry
1 cup water
1 Tbsp. brown sugar

Rub spareribs with 1 tsp. salt. Heat 3 Tbsps. oil, and sauté spareribs until brown. Add soy sauce, sherry, and 1 cup water, cover, and, stirring occasionally, simmer about 20 minutes or until the liquid is almost gone. Turn heat very low, add brown sugar, cover, and cook

until spareribs are completely glazed, stirring occasionally. Served hot or cold. Serves 2 as a main course. Serves 4–8 Chinese style.

Pork with String Beans 肉燉扁豆角
COLOR: PAGE 25

½ lb. lean pork shoulder, thinly sliced and cut in 2-in. lengths
3 Tbsps. oil
½ stalk leek, cut in 1-in. lengths
½ lb. string beans, washed and stringed
3 Tbsps. soy sauce
Pinch salt
1½ cups water

Heat oil, and stir-fry leek until golden. Add pork, and brown quickly; add string beans, and stir-fry briefly. Add soy sauce, salt, and water. Simmer until liquid is absorbed. Serve hot. Serves 2 as a main course. Serves 4–6 Chinese style.

Sweet and Sour Pork Strips 醋溜肉條
COLOR: PAGE 27

½ lb. lean pork (tenderloin or rump), cut in 3 × ½ × 1-in. strips
1 Tbsp. cornstarch mixed with pinch salt
BATTER
    1 egg
    2 Tbsps. flour
Oil for deep frying
SAUCE
    1 Tbsp. dry sherry
    1 Tbsp. soy sauce
    1 tsp. salt
    6 Tbsps. sugar
    2 Tbsps. vinegar
    1 Tbsp. cornstarch
    1 cup water
8 baby tomatoes

Coat pork with cornstarch and salt mixture. Blend egg and flour with egg beater. Heat oil (360°). Dip pork in batter, fry until golden brown, and drain on absorbent paper. Heat sauce ingredients in saucepan on low heat, stirring constantly until thickened. Add fried pork and stir briefly. Remove to serving plate, and decorate with baby tomatoes. Serve hot. Serves 2 as a main course. Serves 4–6 Chinese style.

Pork with Cucumber 肉片炒黄瓜
COLOR: PAGE 27

½ lb. lean pork, cut in 2 × ½-in. slices
MARINADE
    1 tsp. dry sherry
    1 Tbsp. soy sauce
    1 tsp. cornstarch
4 Tbsps. oil
2 cucumbers, washed, and thinly sliced (skinned and seeded if desired)
2 Tbsps. cloud ear mushrooms, soaked in lukewarm water until tender, and hard portions discarded
SEASONINGS
    1 tsp. vinegar
    1 tsp. sugar
    1 Tbsp. soy sauce
    Dash pepper

Mix marinade ingredients, and marinade pork 5 minutes. Heat oil, and stir-fry pork on high heat until just brown. Add cucumber, cloud ear mushrooms, and seasonings, and stir-fry about 1 minute. Serve hot. Serves 2 as a main course. Serves 4–6 Chinese style.

Barbecued Pork 叉燒
COLOR: PAGE 29

2 lbs. pork shoulder, cut in 2 × 4 × 4-in. chunks
MARINADE
    2 Tbsps. soy sauce
    1 Tbsp. Chinese rose wine (if not available, use dry sherry)
    ½ tsp. sesame oil
    4 Tbsps. sugar
    1 tsp. salt
    2 stalks leek, cut in 1-in. lengths
    2 tsps. ginger juice
    2 Tbsps. honey or corn syrup

Mix marinade ingredients, and marinate pork 6 hours. Heat oven to 350°. Roast pork in pan with rack 40–45 minutes, basting frequently with drippings and marinade. Cut in bite-sized pieces, and arrange on plate. Serve hot or at room temperature. Serves 4 as a main course. Serves 6–10 Chinese style.

Note: This barbecued pork can be used as filling for meat buns.

Taking medicine for three years leaves you knowing as much as your doctor.

吃藥三年会行医

Sausage 臘腸
COLOR: PAGE 29

1 lb. pork flank (uncured bacon), meat finely chopped, fat roughly chopped
SEASONINGS
    2 Tbsps. soy sauce
    1 tsp. salt
    1 tsp. sugar
    1 Tbsp. dry sherry
    $\frac{1}{8}$ tsp. powdered five-flavor spice
$\frac{1}{8}$ tsp. saltpeter
1 Tbsp. sesame oil
1 natural sausage skin or 8–10 5-in. plastic sausage skins

Mix pork and seasonings. Tie one end of sausage skin with string, place funnel in open end, and pour in sesame oil to coat the inside and make it slippery. Pack meat mixture tightly for a length of about 5 inches, then tie firmly with string. Puncture all air bubbles that occur while packing by pricking the skin with a needle or toothpick. The sausage skin will seal itself. Take care not to pack meat too tightly. Repeat process until all meat is used. Hang sausage in a very well ventilated place, and let dry 2 weeks. Steam 20 minutes and slice diagonally before serving. Serve hot or at room temperature with shredded leeks and a dip of soy sauce flavored with red pepper oil. Serves 2–3 as a main course. Serves 4–5 Chinese style.

Note: Sausage skins can be ordered from butcher shops. The fresh skins should be washed with salt and alum very carefully. Sausages may also be deep fried about 5 minutes (not with plastic skins).

Fried Pork 炸肉塊
COLOR: PAGE 29

1 lb. boneless pork shoulder, cut in 2-in. cubes
MARINADE
    3 Tbsps. soy sauce
    1 Tbsp. dry sherry
    $\frac{1}{2}$ tsp. ginger juice
    $\frac{1}{4}$ tsp. grated garlic
$\frac{1}{2}$ cup flour
$1\frac{1}{2}$ lightly beaten eggs
1 cup bread crumbs
Oil for deep frying
SAUCE
    $\frac{1}{4}$ cup sugar
    $\frac{1}{2}$ tsp. salt
    1 Tbsp. soy sauce
    $\frac{1}{3}$ cup water

Bring ample amount of water to boil. Add pork, and boil until color changes. Remove pork from water, and soak in marinade 15 minutes. Drain. Reserve marinade. Coat pork with flour, dip in beaten egg, and roll in

bread crumbs. Heat oil to medium (340°), and deep fry pork until golden brown. Remove, and arrange on plate. Keep warm. Mix sauce and marinade ingredients, and simmer on low heat, stirring constantly until mixture thickens. Pour over pork. Serve hot. Serves 2 as a main course. Serves 4-6 Chinese style.

Sweet and Sour Pork 古老肉
COLOR: PAGE 33

1 lb. pork tenderloin, cut in 1-in. cubes
MARINADE
    1 egg yolk
    1 tsp. salt
    1 tsp. soy sauce
    ½ tsp. five-flavor spice (optional)
4 Tbsps. cornstarch
Oil for deep frying
3 Tbsps. oil
1 clove garlic, crushed
1 medium onion, quartered
2 small green peppers, seeded and cut in 1-in. pieces
SEASONINGS
    5 Tbsps. sugar
    5 Tbsps. ketchup
    5 Tbsps. vinegar
2 tsps. cornstarch mixed with ½ cup water
2 slices pineapple, each cut in 6 pieces

Place pork in boiling water 2 minutes. Remove, and pat dry. Mix with marinade, and let stand 15 minutes. Then coat pork with cornstarch. Heat oil (360°), and deep fry pork until light brown. Remove. Drain on absorbent paper. Heat 3 Tbsps. oil, stir-fry garlic, onion, and green pepper on high heat a few minutes, then add seasonings. When just boiling, add cornstarch mixture, stirring constantly until thickened. Add fried pork and pineapple, and stir briefly. Serve hot. Serves 2 as a main course. Serves 4-6 Chinese style.

Note: One fresh red pimento may be substituted for one green pepper.

VEGETABLES

Braised Mushrooms with Asparagus   燴草茹龍鬚菜

COLOR: PAGE 13

1 Tbsp. oil
1 lb. asparagus, hard stems removed, halved, boiled in salted water until tender, and drained
2 Tbsps. oil
2 cups fresh white mushrooms
1 Tbsp. oyster sauce
2 tsps. dry sherry
1 cup soup stock
½ tsp. salt
1 tsp. dry sherry
2 tsps. cornstarch mixed with 2 Tbsps. water

Heat 1 Tbsp. oil, and stir-fry asparagus on high heat until coated with oil. Remove from pan, and arrange on both ends of serving plate. Heat 2 Tbsps. oil, and stir-fry mushrooms on high heat 1 minute. Add oyster sauce and 2 tsps. sherry, and stir-fry until liquid boils. Place mushrooms between asparagus on serving plate. Bring soup stock to boil, and add salt and 1 tsp. sherry. Add cornstarch mixture, and stir constantly until thickened. Pour sauce over mushrooms and asparagus. Serve hot. Serves 2 as a main course. Serves 4–6 Chinese style.

Steamed Stuffed Green Peppers 肉釀青椒

COLOR: PAGE 14

½ lb. ground pork
1 egg
1 stalk leek, chopped roughly
SEASONINGS
    1 Tbsp. dry sherry
    1 tsp. salt
    Dash pepper
    1 tsp. cornstarch
2 green peppers, halved and seeded
1 Tbsp. oil

Mix pork, egg, leek, and seasonings; stuff into 4 green pepper halves. Heat oil, sauté on medium heat, stuffing side down, until browned; then turn, and sauté until green pepper browns slightly. Place on a plate in a steamer, and steam 15 minutes. Serve hot. Serves 2 as a main course. Serves 4 Chinese style.

Marinated Cucumber 鹹黃瓜

COLOR: PAGE 15

1 cucumber, washed, halved lengthwise, seeded, and cut in ½-in. lengths
½ tsp. salt
SEASONINGS
    ½ tsp. sugar
    1 Tbsp. soy sauce
    1 Tbsp. sesame oil

Sprinkle cucumber with salt, and let stand 30 minutes. Drain, and pat dry. Add seasonings, toss, and refrigerate 2 hours. Serve chilled. Serves 2–4 as an hors d'oeuvre or Chinese style.

Chili Turnips 辣萝蔔

COLOR: PAGE 15

1 lb. turnips, quartered and sliced
1 Tbsp. salt
1 2-in. dried red chili pepper, seeded and cut in small rings
1 Tbsp. sugar
1 Tbsp. salt

Sprinkle turnip with salt, toss lightly, and let stand more than 30 minutes. Wash turnip, gently squeeze out water, and let stand 12 hours or overnight. Mix chili pepper, sugar, and salt; add turnip, and toss well. Refrigerate 2 hours. Serve chilled. Serves 4–6 as an hors d'oeuvre or Chinese style.

Pickled Red Radishes

醃小紅蘿蔔

COLOR: PAGE 15

20 red radishes, finely slit through ¾ of length
1 tsp. salt

SEASONINGS
    2 Tbsps. sugar
    1 Tbsp. vinegar
    ½ tsp. salt

Sprinkle slit radishes with salt, and let stand 30 minutes or more. Wash, and gently squeeze out water. Add seasonings, and toss lightly. Refrigerate 3 hours or more. Serve chilled. Serves 5 as an hors d'oeuvre or Chinese style.

Beauty in Bloom

双花比美

COLOR: PAGE 17

1 small cauliflower, washed, flowerets separated, and cut in 1½-in. lengths
1 bunch broccoli, washed, flowerets separated, and cut in 1½-in. lengths
1 tsp. oil
1 tsp. salt
2 Tbsps. oil
1 clove garlic, crushed
½ cup soup stock

SEASONINGS
    ½ tsp. pepper
    1 Tbsp. dry sherry
    1 tsp. sugar
    3 Tbsps. crab roe (dried crab roe available in Chinese groceries)
    ½ tsp. cornstarch mixed with 2 Tbsps. water

Add cauliflower and broccoli to boiling water with 1 tsp. oil and 1 tsp. salt. Boil until not quite tender. Drain. Heat 2 Tbsps. oil, sauté garlic on low heat until golden, and discard. Add soup stock to oil, and then add cauliflower and broccoli. Stir-fry on high heat a few minutes. Remove vegetables, and arrange on serving plate, leaving stock in pan. Add seasonings and crab roe to stock. Add cornstarch mixture, stirring briskly until thickened, and pour over the vegetables on the plate. Serve hot. Serves 2 as a main course. Serves 4–6 Chinese style.

Note: Other fish roe may be substituted if not too salty.

Beancurd with Oyster Sauce 白菌烩豆腐
COLOR: PAGE 17

1 cake beancurd, sliced in 1½-in. squares
½ cup canned *whole white mushrooms*, sliced crosswise
1 Tbsp. green peas, parboiled
3 Tbsps. oil
SEASONINGS
    1 Tbsp. oyster sauce
    1 Tbsp. dry sherry
    ½ tsp. sugar
    ½ tsp. salt
½ cup water

Heat oil, and gently stir-fry beancurd until heated throughout. Add mushroom, green peas, seasonings, and water. Stir by shaking pan gently; cook 2 minutes. Serve hot. Serves 2 as a main course. Serves 2–4 Chinese style.

Fried Stuffed Eggplant 炸茄盒
COLOR: PAGE 18

½ lb. ground pork or beef
3 Tbsps. chopped leek
½ tsp. salt
Dash pepper
1 large eggplant, stemmed, peeled, quartered lengthwise, soaked in water 15 minutes, and cut in ½-in. slices
BATTER
    2 eggs
    1 cup flour
    ½ tsp. salt
    ½ cup water
Oil for deep frying

Mix meat with leek, salt, and pepper. Spread meat filling over one eggplant slice, then cover with another slice. Repeat until all ingredients are used. Mix batter. Dip eggplant into batter. Heat oil to medium (340°), and deep fry eggplant until golden brown. Serve hot with pepper-salt or ketchup as dip. Serves 2 as a main course. Serves 4–6 Chinese style.

Steamed Wintermelon with Ham 蒸冬瓜夾
COLOR: PAGE 21

1 lb. wintermelon, peeled, and cut in 3 × 1 × ¼-in. slices
¼ lb. ham, cut in 3 × ¾-in. slices
SEASONINGS
    1 tsp. salt
    ½ tsp. sugar
    1 tsp. dry sherry

Slit wintermelon slices lengthwise, about ¾ way through, to form a pocket. Insert ham slices in wintermelon. Arrange stuffed slices on a plate, standing on uncut edge (see photo, p. 21). Sprinkle with seasonings, and steam 25 minutes or until tender. Serve hot. Serves 2 as a main course. Serves 4–6 Chinese style.

Stuffed Mushrooms with Sausage 百花齋放
COLOR: PAGE 22

½ lb. ground pork
15 small shrimp, shelled, deveined, and finely chopped
SEASONINGS
    ½ tsp. salt
    Dash pepper
    2 tsps. cornstarch
    2 tsps. sesame oil
9 large, dried Chinese mushrooms, soaked in lukewarm water until tender and stemmed
9 1½-in. pieces of Chinese (see p. 91) or Vienna sausage

Mix pork, shrimp, and seasonings. Stuff mushrooms by filling about 1 ample tablespoon pork mixture in each mushroom cap. Make two ½-in. slits (to quarter) in the end of each sausage piece, and insert uncut end firmly into stuffing mixture on each mushroom (see photo, p. 22). Place stuffed mushrooms on a plate and steam for 15 minutes. While steaming, the slit sausage ends will open up like a flower. Serve hot. Serves 3–4 as an hors d'oeuvre or Chinese style.

Corn Fritters 炸玉米
COLOR: PAGE 22

1 can whole kernel corn, drained
3 Tbsps. green peas
BATTER
    2 eggs
    1 tsp. salt
    ¼ tsp. sugar
    ½ cup flour
Oil for deep frying
Baby tomatoes

Mix batter ingredients, add corn and green peas, and mix. Heat oil (360°), drop corn mixture one tablespoon at a time into oil, and deep fry until golden brown. Decorate with baby tomatoes or parsley. Serve hot. Serves 2 as a main course. Serves 4–6 Chinese style.

Spicy Assorted Vegetables 炒素菜
COLOR: PAGE 22

4 Tbsps. oil
1 clove garlic, crushed
1 cucumber, thinly sliced
2 radishes, thinly sliced
¼ head cabbage, cut in bite-sized pieces
½ carrot, sliced, cut in flower shapes, and parboiled
2 dried mushrooms, soaked in lukewarm water until tender, stemmed, and sliced
SEASONINGS
    1 Tbsp. dry sherry
    2 tsps. soy sauce
    ½ tsp. salt
    ½ tsp. sugar

Heat oil. Brown garlic and discard. Add all the vegetables, and stir-fry briskly 1 minute. Add seasonings, and stir-fry 3 minutes. Serve hot, at room temperature, or chilled. Serves 2 as a main course. Serves 4–6 Chinese style.

Braised Assorted Vegetables 冬茹冬筍燴素菜
COLOR: PAGE 24

3 Tbsps. oil
½ cup canned bamboo shoots, cut in 1½-in. square slices
½ cup dried Chinese mushrooms, soaked in lukewarm water until tender and stemmed
½ head cauliflower, flowerets separated and parboiled
2 stalks brocolli, flowerets separated and parboiled
5 slices carrot, cut in star shapes and parboiled
5–6 cobs canned baby corn
12 snow peas, washed and stringed
¼ cup canned or fresh white mushrooms, sliced
¼ cup canned gingko nuts
2 Tbsps. green peas, parboiled
SEASONINGS
   ½ tsp. salt
   1 tsp. dry sherry
   Dash pepper
1 cup soup stock
1 tsp. cornstarch mixed with 2 Tbsps. water

Heat oil, and stir-fry all vegetables 3 minutes. Add seasonings, and stir-fry briefly. Add soup stock, and just bring to boil. Add cornstarch mixture, and stir until thickened. Serve hot. Serves 2 as a main course. Serves 4–6 Chinese style.

Sautéed Beancurd with Mushrooms 紅燒豆腐
COLOR: PAGE 26

1 cake beancurd, sprinkled with 1 tsp. salt, cut in 8 pieces, and patted dry
1 Tbsp. cornstarch
4 Tbsps. oil
1 clove garlic, crushed
2 stalks leek, cut in 4-in. lengths
6 oz. pork, cut in bite-sized slices
3 dried Chinese mushrooms, soaked in lukewarm water until tender and stemmed
SEASONINGS
   1 Tbsp. dry sherry
   ½ tsp. sugar
   3 Tbsps. soy sauce

Sprinkle beancurd with cornstarch. Heat 2 Tbsps. oil, and sauté beancurd on high heat until golden, taking care not to break up beancurd. Remove, and set aside. Heat another 2 Tbsps. oil, brown garlic on medium heat, and discard. Add leek, pork and mushrooms, and stir-fry 1 minute. Add beancurd and seasonings, reduce heat to low, and stir (by shaking pan) 3 minutes. Serve hot. Serves 2 as a main course. Serves 2–4 Chinese style.

Note: If desired, use 2 Tbsps. oyster sauce instead of soy sauce.

Green Peppers and Bean Sprouts 炒銀芽青椒
COLOR: PAGE 27

½ lb. lean pork, shredded
2 tsps. soy sauce
2 tsps. dry sherry
1 tsp. cornstarch
1 lb. bean sprouts, washed, drained, and roots removed
1 green pepper, washed, seeded, and sliced in rings
3 Tbsps. oil
½ tsp. salt
1 tsp. vinegar

Mix pork with soy sauce, sherry, and cornstarch. Heat oil, and stiry-fry pork on medium heat until browned. Add bean sprouts and green pepper, and stir-fry 1 minute on high heat. Add salt and vinegar. Remove to plate quickly, and serve immediately. Serves 2 as a main course. Serves 4–6 Chinese style.

Assorted Vegetables with Black Pickles 炒鹹菜丁
COLOR: PAGE 28

½ lb. pork, diced
5 Tbsps. oil
½ medium carrot, skinned, diced, and parboiled
½ cup diced canned bamboo shoots
2 Tbsps. green peas, parboiled
¼ cup salted black turnip pickle, washed and diced
2 Tbsps. soy sauce
1 Tbsp. sugar

Heat oil, and stir-fry pork, vegetables, and pickle 2 minutes. Add soy sauce and sugar, and stir-fry 1 minute. Serve hot or at room temperature. Serves 2 as a main course. Serves 4–6 Chinese style.

Note: Black pickles are written 大頭鹹菜 in Chinese and are available either canned or fresh in Chinese food shops. Fresh turnips may be substituted.

When the man farms and the woman weaves, there is enough to wear and to eat.

男勤耕，女勤織足衣又足食

Spicy Salad 炒素菜
COLOR: PAGE 29

4 medium turnips, thinly sliced in 2 × 1-in. rectangles and parboiled
1 medium carrot, sliced lengthwise in 2 × 1-in. rectangles and parboiled
2 Tbsps. oil
2 small cucumbers, sliced lengthwise in 2 × 1-in. rectangles
1 green pepper, seeded and cut in rings
½ medium onion, sliced vertically
1 clove garlic, finely chopped
2 dried red chili peppers, seeded and cut in 4 pieces
2 cups water

SEASONINGS
    1 Tbsp. vinegar
    1 tsp. salt
    2 tsps. sugar

Soak parboiled turnip and carrot in cold water for 1 minute. Drain, and pat dry. Heat oil, and stir-fry all ingredients, including seasonings, for 2 minutes. Cool to room temperature and chill in refrigerator (may be kept in refrigerator for up to 3 days). Serve chilled. Serves 2 as a salad course. Serves 4 Chinese style.

Chilled Cucumber 涼黃瓜
COLOR: PAGE 29

1 cucumber, quartered lengthwise, crushed with a kitchen mallet or bottle, and cut in 3-in. lengths (peeled if desired)
1 tsp. salt
1 2-in. dried red chili pepper, seeded and cut in 4 pieces
1 Tbsp. sesame oil

Sprinkle cucumber with salt and red chili pepper. Refrigerate at least 30 minutes. Sprinkle with sesame oil before serving. Serves 2–4 as an hors d'oeuvre or Chinese style.

Crisp Peanuts 炸花生
COLOR: PAGE 29

1 cup peanuts
Oil for deep frying
Pinch salt

Heat ample oil to low (320°), and deep fry peanuts until golden brown. Remove from oil as soon as color changes, since peanuts scorch easily. Sprinkle with salt. Serve at room temperature. Serves 4–6 as a snack.

Note: Either skinned or unskinned peanuts may be used.

Spicy Lima Beans
五香蚕豆

COLOR: PAGE 29

1 lb. large lima beans, fresh or frozen
2 Tbsps. oil
1 dried red chili pepper, seeded and cut in 3 pieces
1 Tbsps. sugar
1 clove star anise
½ tsp. salt

Heat oil, and stir-fry lima beans a few minutes. Add chili pepper, sugar, and star anise, and stir 1 minute. Add water to cover, add salt, cover, and cook on medium heat until liquid disappears. Serve hot or at room temperature. Serves 4–6 as an hors d'oeuvre or Chinese style.

Rice is for the hungry; talk is for friends.

飯送給飢人，話說給知人

Deep Fried Eggs 翡翠果

COLOR: PAGE 19

6 eggs, hard-boiled and shelled
10 quail eggs, hard-boiled and shelled
¾ cup soy sauce
Flour
Oil for deep frying
1 Tbsp. oil
1 lb. spinach, washed, stems removed, and cut in 3-in. lengths
1 tsp. salt

Soak hard-boiled eggs in soy sauce 15 minutes, turning occasionally. Coat eggs lightly with flour. Heat oil to medium (340°), and deep fry eggs until golden brown. Remove and drain. Heat 1 Tbsp. oil, and stir-fry spinach briefy with salt. Arrange fried eggs on top of or beside spinach on serving plate. Serve hot. Serves 3 as a main course. Serves 6 Chinese style.

Note: Do not overcook spinach, or it will loose its greenness.

Forest Eggs 木須蛋
COLOR: PAGE 27

4 eggs
1 tsp. salt
½ cup cloud ear mushrooms, soaked in lukewarm water until tender and hard portions discarded
4 Tbsps. oil

Beat eggs lightly with salt, and add cloud ear mushrooms. Heat oil, and scramble egg mixture on high heat until just firm. Serve hot. Serves 2 as a main course. Serves 4–6 Chinese style.

Scrambled Eggs with Crabmeat 蟹肉炒蛋
COLOR: PAGE 33

4 eggs
1 tsp. salt
Dash pepper
¾ cup canned or frozen crabmeat, cartilage removed, and broken in shreds
4 Tbsps. oil

Beat eggs lightly, add salt, pepper, and crabmeat, and mix well. Heat oil, and stir-fry egg and crab mixture until just firm. Serve hot. Serves 2 as a main course. Serves 4–6 Chinese style.

RICE, NOODLES, AND BREAD

Fried Rice with Assorted Meat 什錦炒飯
COLOR: PAGE 28

4 cups cold, cooked rice
4 Tbsps. oil
2 eggs, beaten lightly with pinch of salt
½ cup diced chicken meat
½ cup diced shrimp
2 slices ham, diced
3 Tbsps. chopped leek, or onion
¼ cup diced canned bamboo shoots
1 or 2 dried Chinese mushrooms, soaked in lukewarm water until tender, stemmed, and diced
¼ cup green peas, parboiled
½ tsp. salt
Dash pepper

Heat 1 Tbsp. oil, and scramble egg mixture. Remove and set aside. Heat remaining oil in pan, and stir-fry chicken, shrimp, ham, leek, bamboo shoot, and mushroom until chicken is done. Add rice, and stir-fry with a wooden spatula or spoon. Mix ingredients well to bring out the flavors fully. Add scrambled egg, green peas, salt, and pepper, and stir. Serve hot. Serves 2 as a main dish. Serves 4 Chinese style.

Note: Take care not to mash the rice, but keep the grains whole while frying.

Abalone and Chicken Congee 鮑魚粥
COLOR: PAGE 34

½ cup rice, washed
8 cups water
½ cup shredded, canned abalone
½ cup shredded, boiled chicken
Pinch salt
1 Tbsp. green peas
Soy sauce
Sesame oil

Place rice in a deep pan. Add 8 cups water, bring to boil, cover, and simmer 20 minutes. Add shredded abalone, chicken, and salt (to taste), and simmer 15 minutes. Add green peas, and continue cooking 3 minutes more. Remove from heat, and serve hot. Season with soy sauce and sesame oil to taste before eating. Serves 1.

Note: Generally the depth of flavor of congee increases with cooking time. This dish may be reheated before serving.

Fried Wonton 炸餛飩
COLOR: PAGE 26

1 cup all-purpose flour
1 egg, beaten
Pinch salt
½ cup shrimp, shelled, deveined, and finely chopped
2 Tbsps. pork fat, finely chopped
SEASONINGS
    1 Tbsp. dry sherry
    1 tsp. salt
    ½ tsp. sugar
    Dash pepper
Oil for deep frying

Add egg to flour, and mix well. Knead dough until smooth, wrap in damp cloth, and set aside for 30 minutes. With rolling pin roll out dough to semitransparent thickness, and cut in 3 × 3-inch squares. Sprinkle squares with cornstarch to prevent sticking, and stack. (To store, wrap stacks of wrappings in foil or wax paper, and refrigerate.) Mix shrimp, pork fat, and seasonings. Place wrapping square with corner towards you, dip fingertip in water, and moisten opposite edge. Place ½ tsp. filling in center of wrapping, fold corner across to opposite corner (corners should not align exactly), and pleat as shown in process photos, page 109. Press pleats gently but firmly to seal. Heat oil (360°), and deep fry until golden. Serve hot or at room temperature as an hors d'oeuvre. Makes 20 wonton.

Note: Ready-made wrappings may be purchased at Chinese foodstores or restaurants.

Spring Rolls 炸春捲
COLOR: PAGE 34

½ lb. lean pork, shredded
MARINADE
    1 Tbsp. soy sauce
    1 Tbsp. dry sherry
    1 tsp. cornstarch
4 Tbsps. oil
1 cup shredded cabbage
1 green pepper, seeded and shredded
1 Tbsp. soy sauce
½ tsp. salt
2 tsps. cornstarch mixed with 2 Tbsps. water
20 spring roll wrappings (ready-made)
1 Tbsp. flour mixed with 1½ Tbsps. water

Mix marinade, and marinate pork 10 minutes. Heat oil, and stir-fry pork until color changes. Add cabbage and green pepper, and stir-fry 2 minutes. Add 1 Tbsp. soy sauce and ½ tsp. salt, and stir-fry 2 minutes more. Add cornstarch mixture and stir until thickened. Remove and cool. Place 2 Tbsps. filling in the lower third of a wrapping to within 1 inch of the edges (see process photos, p. 109). Roll once, fold in both edges, moisten edge with flour-water mixture, and roll completely. Place on plate with sealed edge down. Heat oil (360°), and deep fry until golden. Serve hot. Makes 20 rolls.

Crisp Fried Noodles with Spinach 菠菜炸麵
COLOR: PAGE 32

Oil for deep frying
1 lb. package dried Chinese noodles (or 3 cups fresh noodles), cooked
½ cup shredded lean beef or pork
MARINADE
    1 Tbsp. dry sherry
    2 tsps. soy sauce
    1 tsp. cornstarch
3 Tbsps. oil
½ cup shredded canned bamboo shoots
½ bunch young spinach, washed and stems removed
SEASONINGS
    1 Tbsp. dry sherry
    2 Tbsps. soy sauce
    ½ tsp. salt
    ¼ tsp. sugar
1 cup soup stock
½ Tbsp. cornstarch mixed with 1 Tbsp. water

Heat oil to low (320°), and deep fry noodles until crisp. Drain on absorbent paper. Mix marinade, and marinate meat 10 minutes. Heat 3 Tbsps. oil, and stir-fry meat until color changes. Add bamboo shoot and spinach, and stir-fry 1 minute. Add seasonings and soup stock, and bring just to boil. Add cornstarch mixture, and stir until thickened. Pour mixture over noodles. Serve hot. Serves 2 as a main course. Serves 3–4 Chinese style.

Soft Fried Noodles with Shrimp 蝦仁炒麵
COLOR: PAGE 32

3 Tbsps. oil
1 lb. package dried Chinese noodles (or 3 cups fresh noodles), cooked, and mixed with 1 Tbsp. sesame oil
1 cup small shrimp, shelled and deveined
MARINADE
    1 Tbsp. dry sherry
    $\frac{1}{2}$ tsp. salt
    1 tsp. cornstarch
2 Tbsps. oil
$\frac{1}{4}$ cup canned bamboo shoots, cut in bite-sized pieces
$\frac{1}{2}$ stalk leek, cut in $\frac{1}{2}$-in. lengths
SEASONINGS
    1 Tbsp. dry sherry
    2 Tbsps. soy sauce
    $\frac{1}{2}$ tsp. salt
    $\frac{1}{4}$ tsp. sugar
1 cup soup stock
1 Tbsp. green peas, parboiled
$\frac{1}{2}$ Tbsp. cornstarch mixed with 1 Tbsp. water

Heat 3 Tbsps. oil, add cooked noodles, and fry (without stirring) on medium heat until brown on bottom. Turn, and brown other side. A little oil may be added when noodles are turned. Remove to serving plate. Mix marinade, and marinate shrimp 5 minutes. Heat 2 Tbsps. oil, and stir-fry shrimp until just pink. Add bamboo shoot and leek, and stir-fry on high heat 1 minute. Add seasonings and soup stock, and bring just to boil. Add green peas and cornstarch mixture, and stir until thickened. Pour mixture over noodles, and serve hot. Serves 2 as a main course. Serves 3-4 Chinese style.

Egg Noodles 鶏蛋麺
COLOR: PAGE 33

2 cups all-purpose flour
2 eggs
Pinch salt

Beat eggs lightly; mix with flour until smooth, adding a little water if necessary. Knead dough until soft. Cover dough with damp cloth, and let stand 20 minutes. Knead again. On a lightly floured board, roll out dough into a $\frac{1}{8}$-$\frac{1}{6}$ inch-thick sheet with a rolling pin. (The thinner the sheet, the finer the noodles). Arrange the sheet in accordion folds to make 4 or 5 pleats or layers (see process photos, p. 110). Cut across the folds in $\frac{1}{8}$-inch widths, to make long, thin strands. The fresh, homemade noodles may be boiled and served in broth (see pp. 113-14) or be boiled, fried, and topped by meat, shrimp, etc. (see p. 107, right). Serves 1 as a main course. Serves 2-3 Chinese style.

14-16. filling wonton (p. 106)

15.

16.

17-18. filling spring rolls (p. 107)

18.

109

19–21. cutting noodles (pp. 108, 113)

20.

21.

22–29. dumplings (pp. 114–16)

23.

24.

25.

26.

27.

28.

29.

30–36. flower buns (p. 116)   32.   33.

34.   35.   36.

Spinach Noodles 菠菜麵
COLOR: PAGE 33

1 bunch spinach, washed and finely chopped
1½ tsps. salt
2 cups all-purpose flour

Sprinkle chopped spinach with salt, place in cheesecloth, and squeeze firmly to extract juice. This should give about ½ cup juice. (Or obtain ½ cup juice by liquifying spinach in a blender and straining juice through cheesecloth.) Sift flour into a bowl, mix with spinach juice until smooth, and knead until soft. The following process is exactly the same as that for Egg Noodles, page 108. Serves 1 as a main course. Serves 2–3 Chinese style.

Note: If ½ cup spinach juice is not obtained from the amount of spinach specified, water may be added.

Noodles with Shrimp 蝦仁湯麵
COLOR: PAGE 33

1 lb. package dried Chinese noodles (or 3 cups fresh egg noodles), cooked
2 Tbsps. oil
½ lb. medium shrimp, shelled and deveined
½ tsp. salt
1 tsp. cornstarch
2 cups chicken soup stock
Dash pepper
Pinch salt
1 stalk spinach, washed, stems removed, parboiled, and cut in 4-in. lengths

Place cooked noodles in serving bowl. Mix shrimp with salt and cornstarch. Heat oil, and stir-fry shrimp until just pink. Arrange on top of noodles. Heat stock, season to taste, and pour in noodle bowl. Place spinach beside shrimp. Serve hot. Serves 2 as a main course. Serves 3–4 Chinese style.

When someone talks, listen to his voice; when eating vegetables, eat the hearts.

听話要呼音，吃菜要吃心

Noodles with Chicken   鶏絲湯麵
COLOR: PAGE 33

1 lb. package dried Chinese noodles (or 3 cups fresh spinach noodles), cooked
½ lb. chicken breast (with bone)
3 slices fresh ginger
½ stalk leek
2 cups chicken stock
Dash pepper
Pinch salt

Place noodles in serving bowl. Boil chicken with ginger and leek in enough water to cover until tender, then bone and shred. Reserve broth for use as stock. Arrange shredded chicken on noodles. Heat 2 cups stock, season to taste, and pour in noodle bowl. Serve hot. Serves 2 as a main course. Serves 3–4 Chinese style.

Note: Roast chicken may be substituted for boiled.

Steamed Dumplings   蒸餃
COLOR: PAGE 33

2 cups all-purpose flour
⅔ cup boiling water (approximately, depending on brand of flour)
½ lb. ground pork
¼ lb. shrimp, shelled, deveined, and finely chopped
SEASONINGS
    Greens of 4 green onions or scallions, finely chopped
    2 Tbsps. soy sauce
    ½ tsp. salt
    3 Tbsps. sesame oil

Sift flour into bowl. Add boiling water, and mix until firm. Knead dough on lightly floured board until smooth. Wrap in a damp cloth, and let stand at least 20 minutes. Knead dough again, and roll out into a long sausage 1½ inches in diameter (see process photos, pp. 110–11). Cut in 1½-inch slices. Flatten each slice with palm of hand, and with rolling pin roll out into very thin rounds about 3 inches in diameter. Mix shrimp, pork, and seasonings. Place 2 tsps. filling in center of wrapping, and fold into half circle, then pleat and pinch the edges together as illustrated in the process photos. Place dumplings on a damp cloth in a steamer, and steam 15 minutes. Serve hot with red pepper oil, vinegar, and soy sauce, to be combined by the diner as a dip. Makes 24 dumplings.

Fried Dumplings 鍋貼
COLOR: PAGE 33

3 cups all-purpose flour
1 cup boiling water (approximately, depending on brand of flour)
½ lb. ground pork
¼ lb. shrimp, shelled, deveined, and finely chopped
SEASONINGS
    1 tsp. grated fresh ginger
    2 Tbsps. soy sauce
    ½ tsp. salt
    2 Tbsps. sesame or salad oil
    1 Tbsp. dry sherry
3 Tbsps. oil

Sift flour into bowl. Add boiling water, and mix until firm. Knead dough on lightly floured board until smooth. Wrap in damp cloth, and let stand at least 20 minutes. Knead dough again, and roll out into a long sausage 1½ inches in diameter (see process photos, pp. 110-11). Cut in ½-inch slices. Flatten each slice with palm of hand, and with rolling pin roll out into very thin rounds about 3 inches in diameter. Mix shrimp, pork, and seasonings. Place 2 tsps. filling in center of wrapping, and fold into half circle, then pleat and pinch the edges together as illustrated in the process photos. Arrange dumplings in rows of six or seven on a plate. Taking care that the heat is in direct contact with the entire pan bottom, heat oil to medium, and with a spatula place one or two dumpling rows in pan, sealed edges up. Fry until light brown. Add water to cover two-thirds height of dumplings, cover pan, and cook over medium heat until water evaporates (8-10 minutes). Serve hot with red pepper oil, vinegar, and soy sauce, to be combined by the diner as a dip. Makes 30 dumplings.

Shrimp Dumplings 蝦餃
COLOR: PAGE 34

3 cups all-purpose flour
1 cup boiling water (approximately, depending on brand of flour)
½ lb. ground pork
¼ lb. shrimp, shelled, deveined, and finely chopped
SEASONINGS
    1 tsp. ginger juice
    2 tsps. soy sauce
    1 tsp. dry sherry
    3 tsps. sesame oil
    ½ tsp. salt

Sift flour into bowl. Add boiling water, and mix until firm. Knead dough on lightly floured board until smooth. Wrap in damp cloth, and let stand at least 20 minutes. Knead dough again, and roll out into a long sausage 1½ inches in diameter (see process photos, pp.

110–11). Cut in ½-inch slices. Flatten each slice with palm of hand, and with rolling pin roll out into very thin rounds about 3 inches in diameter. Mix shrimp, pork, and seasonings. Place 1½ tsps. filling in center of wrapping, and fold into half circle, then pleat and pinch the edges together as illustrated in the process photos. Place dumplings on a damp cloth in a steamer, and steam 15 minutes. Serve hot with red pepper oil, vinegar, and soy sauce, to be combined by the diner as a dip. Makes 40 small dumplings.

Note: There are many ways to pleat and seal dumplings. You may wish to create a different, attractive pleat shape for each of the three varieties of dumpling included in this book.

Steamed Flower Buns 花 卷
COLOR: PAGE 34

1½ tsps. dry yeast
1 tsp. sugar
½ cup warm water
3 cups all-purpose flour
Pinch salt
2 Tbsps. sugar
2 tsps. baking powder
2 Tbsps. sesame oil
½ tsp. salt

Dissolve yeast in warm water with 1 tsp. sugar. Sift flour with salt and 2 Tbsps. sugar. When yeast begins to bubble, add to sifted flour, mix until firm, and knead on a lightly floured board until dough is smooth. Place dough in a bowl, cover with a damp cloth, and let stand for 3 hours. When the dough has risen, add baking powder, and knead again on a lightly floured board. With a rolling pin roll out into a ⅛-inch-thick sheet. Brush with sesame oil, and sprinkle with salt. Then roll up like a jelly roll into a 2-inch diameter. Cut the roll in 1-inch lengths. Take two slices of dough roll, and hold together on the skin side (see process photos, p. 112). Gently stretch while twisting the ends in opposite directions at the same time, twisting each end 180°, until the center of each roll slice extends out like a rosebud. Pinch the ends into the dough, and place on a damp cloth in a steamer with the pinched ends down. This twisting and stretching process should be done gently but rapidly, and in one motion; a little experimentation may be necessary before best results are achieved. Serve hot as bread with meal. Makes 12 buns.

37–49. silver strand rolls (p. 119)   38.   39.

40.   41.   42.

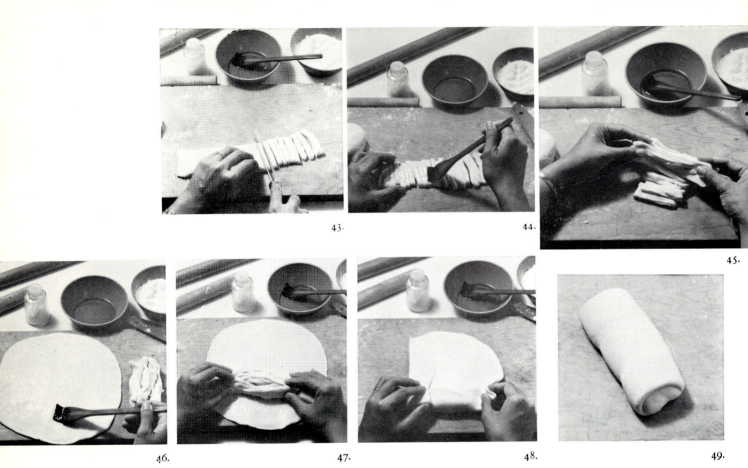

43. 44. 45.
46. 47. 48. 49.

Steamed Silver Strand Rolls 銀絲卷

COLOR: PAGE 34

1½ tsps. dry yeast
1 tsp. sugar
½ cup warm water
3 cups all-purpose flour
Pinch salt
2 Tbsps. sugar
2 tsps. baking powder
2 Tbsps. sesame seed oil
½ tsp. salt

Dissolve yeast in warm water with 1 tsp. sugar. Sift flour with salt and 2 Tbsps. sugar. When yeast begins to bubble, add to sifted flour, mix until firm, and knead on a lightly floured board until dough is smooth. Place dough in a bowl, cover with a damp cloth, and let stand for 3 hours. When the dough has risen, add baking powder, and knead again on a lightly floured board. Divide dough into 4 parts. With a rolling pin roll out ¼ of the dough into a ⅛-inch-thick round. Brush with oil, then fold into 3 layers. Cut into ⅓-inch widths. Brush with oil again and stretch slightly (see process photos, p. 117) into strands. Roll another ¼ of dough into ⅛-inch-thick round. Brush with oil, sprinkle with salt, and place the bundle of dough strands on bottom half of round. Roll once, fold in both edges, and roll completely. Repeat process for remaining half of dough. Place on damp cloth in steamer, and steam for 15–20 minutes. Cut each roll in half while hot and serve hot as bread with meal. Serves 4.

SOUPS

Corn Soup with Ground Chicken 鷄茸粟米湯
COLOR: PAGE 18

¼ lb. ground chicken
1 egg white
1 tsp. dry sherry
Dash pepper
1 tsp. salt
1 can sweet corn, undrained
6 cups chicken stock
Pinch salt
Dash pepper
2 Tbsps. cornstarch mixed with 4 Tbsps. water
1 egg, beaten lightly
1 tsp. chopped parsley
1 tsp. chopped ham

Mix ground chicken with egg white, sherry, pepper, and salt in bowl. Add sweet corn, and mix well. Bring chicken stock to boil. Add ground chicken and sweet corn mixture slowly, stirring constantly. Season with salt and pepper to taste. When stock boils again, thicken with cornstarch mixture. Then add beaten egg slowly, stirring constantly. Pour into soup tureen, and sprinkle with chopped parsley and ham. Serve hot. Serves 2 as a soup course. Serves 3–6 Chinese style.

Beef in Yunnan Pot   雲南汽鍋牛肉
COLOR: PAGE 20

½ lb. lean beef, cut in 1 × 2-in. slices
1 cup dried Chinese mushrooms, soaked in lukewarm water until tender, stemmed, and quartered
1 cup canned bamboo shoots, cut in bite-sized pieces
5 cups soup stock
1 stalk leek, cut in 1-in. lengths
4 slices fresh ginger
1 tsp. dry sherry
1 tsp. salt
Dash pepper

Bring ample amount of water in large saucepan to boil. Add beef, mushroom, and bamboo shoot. Bring to boil again, remove from heat, and drain. Discard boiling water. Pour soup stock into Yunnan pot; add leek, ginger, beef, mushroom, bamboo shoot, and all seasonings. Cover, place pot in a steamer, and steam about 2–3 hours. Serve hot. Serves 2 as a soup course. Serves 4–5 Chinese style.

Note: A Yunnan pot is a lidded earthenware casserole with a closed, pointed chimney rising through the center to the lid to distribute heat more evenly. A good Duch oven or casserole may be substituted.

Chinese Cabbage and Mushroom Soup   白菜冬茹湯
COLOR: PAGE 27

MEATBALLS
   ¼ lb. ground pork
   2 tsps. finely chopped leek
   2 tsps. dry sherry
   ½ tsp. salt
   1 tsp. soy sauce
   1 tsp. sesame oil
   1½ tsps. cornstarch
Oil for deep frying
5 cups soup stock
⅓ lb. Chinese cabbage, washed and cut in bite-sized pieces
8 dried Chinese mushrooms, soaked in lukewarm water until tender and stemmed
SEASONINGS
   1½ tsps. salt
   1 Tbsp. dry sherry
   Dash pepper

Mix ingredients for meatballs, and form into walnut-sized balls. Heat oil (360°), deep fry meatballs until golden, and drain on absorbent paper. Bring soup stock to boil, add meatballs, Chinese cabbage, and mushrooms, and simmer uncovered until vegetables are tender. Add seasonings, and serve hot. Serves 2 as a soup course. Serves 4–6 Chinese style.

Shrimp Ball Soup 蝦丸湯
COLOR: PAGE 31

½ lb. shrimp, shelled, deveined, and finely chopped with 2 Tbsps. water
1 tsp. dry sherry
1 tsp. salt
1 Tbsp. cornstarch
5 cups soup stock
4 leaves Chinese cabbage, cut in 3-in. pieces
1½ tsps. salt
1 Tbsp. dry sherry
Dash pepper

Mix shrimp with sherry, salt, and cornstarch. Wet hands, and form walnut-sized balls of about 1 Tbsp. shrimp mixture. Place on a plate. Bring soup stock to boil, add shrimp balls and Chinese cabbage. Cover, and simmer until tender (10 minutes). Add salt, sherry, and pepper to taste; serve hot. Serves 2 as a soup course. Serves 4-5 Chinese style.

Note: If desired, dried Chinese mushrooms, soaked in lukewarm water until tender, stemmed, and halved, may be added to boiling soup stock with shrimp balls.

Watercress Soup 牛肉西洋菜湯
COLOR: PAGE 31

½ lb. beef shank
3 carrot slices for decoration
6 cups water
1 Tbsp. oil
½ lb. watercress
Pinch salt

Put beef and carrot in 6 cups water, bring to boil, and simmer until beef is tender. Remove beef, slice or cube, and return to soup. Heat oil until fuming, and stir-fry watercress briefly, until color becomes bright green. Add watercress while soup is boiling, and add salt to taste. Remove from heat when soup comes to boil again after adding watercress. Serves 2 as a soup course. Serves 4-6 Chinese style.

Note: Watercress must be added to boiling water or soup, otherwise it will be bitter.

Clam Soup　　　蛤蜊湯
COLOR: PAGE 32

2 dozen baby clams
1 Tbsp. green peas
4 cups water or clam nectar
SEASONINGS
 1 Tbsp. dry sherry
 1 tsp. salt
 Dash pepper

Soak clams in salted water to cover 2–4 hours. An iron nail placed in the water will make the clams discharge all sand. Add clams and green peas to boiling water or clam nectar, and boil on high heat until clams open. Add seasonings, and bring just to boil again. Serve immediately. Serves 2 as a soup course. Serves 2–4 Chinese style.

Cantonese Firepot　　　火鍋子
COLOR: PAGE 30

The firepot is a type of chafing dish with a central chimney into which lighted charcoal is placed to keep the broth simmering while dining. An ordinary, large chafing dish or a casserole over a hotplate may be substituted, but in this case the soup stock should be brought to a quick boil first in the kitchen.

All advance preparation should be completed in the kitchen. The diners are seated around the firepot in the center of the table and, with chopsticks or a long-handled fork, cook their own choice of the numerous thinly sliced ingredients by placing them in the simmering soup stock briefly and removing them to their own plates. Each diner seasons his own food with his choice of four different condiments, which are combined in the diner's soup bowl.

Soup stock should be added if the level falls much below half full, and lighted charcoal may be added occasionally. A light, clear chicken stock should be used, or one may prefer to start with just water. The stock becomes richer as the flavors of the various ingredients are added. At the end of the meal the remaining full-flavored broth may be eaten with rice or noodles.

UTENSILS
 Dinner plate
 Deep soup bowl or cereal bowl (for condiments and soup)

Soup spoon
Chopsticks or long-handled fork
Wire mesh dipper (tea strainer may be used)

INGREDIENTS

½ lb. beef, cut in paper-thin slices
½ lb. lean pork, cut in paper-thin slices
½ lb. white meat fish, cut in ⅛-in.-thick slices
½ lb. large scallops, cut in ⅛-in.-thick slices
½ lb. shrimp, shelled and deveined
½ lb. abalone, cut in paper-thin slices
½ lb. oysters, cleaned and parboiled
½ lb. beef liver, cut in ⅛-in.-thick slices and parboiled
½ lb. chicken fillet, cut in ⅛-in.-thick slices
crabmeat balls: 1 can crabmeat mixed with 1 egg and 2 Tbsps. cornstarch, formed into walnut-sized balls and parboiled
½ lb. pork tripe, cleaned and boiled 40 minutes
½ lb. cuttlefish, cleaned, legs, head, and skin removed, and cut in ⅛-in.-thick slices
2 cakes beancurd, sliced
½ head Chinese cabbage, cut in bite-sized pieces
2 bunches spinach, washed, stems and tough leaves removed, and cut in bite-sized pieces
1 package transparent vermicelli, soaked in lukewarm water until soft
10 shrimp balls (see recipe, p. 122)
1 raw egg per diner

CONDIMENTS

¼ cup vinegar
¼ cup soy sauce
½ cup chopped leek
5 Tbsps. red pepper oil or tabasco sauce

Keep condiment bowls on table filled.

The pleasure of a firepot meal is not only in the eating, but also in the friendship and warmth that comes with sharing good food together. Though the pun was not intentional, one Chinese lady expressed this eloquently: "Keep the stock bubbling then gets the good atmosphere." Serves 8–10.

DESSERTS

Glazed Sweet Potatoes 拔絲白薯
COLOR: PAGE 35

1 lb. sweet potatoes, peeled, cut in bite-sized pieces, soaked in water 5 minutes, drained, and wiped dry
Oil for deep frying
3 Tbsps. oil
¾ cup sugar
1 Tbsp. oil

Heat oil to medium (340°), and deep fry sweet potato until light brown. Remove, and drain on absorbent paper. Bring 3 Tbsps. water to boil, and add sugar and oil. Simmer, stirring constantly, until mixture thickens and forms a ball when a bit is dropped into cold water. Add fried sweet potato, and stir until pieces are completely glazed. Remove to plate, and serve hot with a bowl of ice water. Dip each piece into ice water before eating. Serves 2 as a dessert course. Serves 4–6 Chinese style.

Note: The hot glaze should form threads as the sweet potato is coated.

Stuffed Apples   釀苹果
COLOR: PAGE 35

1 cup glutinous rice
1½ cups water
½ cup finely chopped pineapple
4 Tbsps. dried or canned lotus seeds
4 Tbsps. finely chopped canned lily root (optional)
4 Tbsps. sugar
4 apples, washed, topped, and cored; 2 apples peeled, (see photo, p. 35)
16 green peas
4 cherries

Wash rice, and rinse until water is clear. Add water to rice, cover saucepan, bring to boil, and simmer 30 minutes or until water is absorbed. Mix cooked rice with pineapple, lotus seeds, lily root, and sugar. Stuff apples with rice mixture, and decorate with green peas and cherries. Steam 15 minutes. Remove. Serve hot or cold. Serves 4 as a dessert course or Chinese style.

Note: Blanched almonds, roughly slivered, may be substituted for lotus seeds. Diced sweet chestnuts may be substituted for lily root.

Fruit Compote   水果汁
COLOR: PAGE 35

4 cups water
3 Tbsps. sugar
2 pineapple slices, quartered
½ cup canned mandarin oranges
6 canned water chestnuts, sliced
12 strawberries, halved

Place water and sugar in saucepan, and heat until sugar dissolves. Remove and cool. Add remaining ingredients, and mix. Serve chilled. Serves 2 as a dessert course. Serves 4–6 Chinese style.

126

Stuffed Sweet Lotus 糖連藕

COLOR: PAGE 35

3 6-in. lotus root sections, peeled, and 1 in. of each end cut off, ends reserved
2 cups glutinous rice, washed and soaked overnight
½ cup sugar

Soak lotus root in water about 10 minutes. With a chopstick or skewer stuff glutinous rice in the lotus root cavities from both ends (see process photo, right). Tap root on cutting board while stuffing to allow rice to fill cavities entirely. Attach cut-off ends, and secure with toothpicks. Place stuffed roots in boiling water to cover, add sugar, bring to boil again, cover, and simmer 1 hour or until the lotus roots are tender. Cut cooked roots in ½-in. slices. Place on serving plate, and top with syrup in which roots were cooked. Serve hot or at room temperature. Serves 10–13 as a dessert course or Chinese style.

Note: If desired, syrup can be thickened with 1 tsp. cornstarch mixed with 1 Tbsp. water.

50. stuffing lotus root sections

Longan and Lichee Compote 荔枝桂圓汁

COLOR: PAGE 36

4 cups water
4 Tbsps. sugar
1½ dozen dried longans, shelled
2 dozen fresh or canned lichees

Bring 4 cups water to boil. Add sugar and dried longans. Simmer 10 minutes. Add lichees, and continue cooking 5 minutes. Serve hot or cold. Serves 4 as a dessert course or Chinese style.

Sesame Puffs

COLOR: PAGE 36

炸煎堆

½ cup brown sugar
1 cup water
3 cups glutinous rice flour
⅓ cup white sesame seeds
Oil for deep frying

This confection is usually served at Chinese New Year, the swelling of the balls signifying good luck. A trickier but delicious variation is to fill the dough balls with sweet bean jam. This requires more care when pressing the balls while frying.

Dissolve brown sugar in water. Mix in glutinous rice flour, and blend until smooth and firm. Form the dough into large walnut-sized balls. Roll balls in sesame seeds until fully coated. Heat oil to medium (340°), and place 3 or 4 balls in oil. Press each ball briefly and firmly against the bottom of the pan with a long-handled spoon (see process photo, right). This process must be continuous to allow the balls to swell evenly. When the balls float to the surface, increase the heat and continue the pressing process until the balls have increased about three times in size. Be careful not to overheat the oil. Remove and drain on absorbent paper. Serve hot or at room temperature as a dessert. Makes 24 puffs.

51. pressing sesame puffs while deep frying

Note: Pressing the balls of dough while frying is a bit tricky at first, and a few experimental trials with single balls are recommended. Let the balls fry about 30 seconds before pressing, or the dough will stick to the spoon. Turn the balls constantly (chopsticks are convenient) and press from all sides to insure an even shape. Do not press after the skin has become firm and golden.

Almond Float 杏仁豆腐

COLOR: PAGE 36

1 stick agar-agar or 2–3 envelopes gelatin
2 cups water
4 Tbsps. sugar
1 cup milk
1 Tbsp. almond extract
2 cups canned fruit salad with syrup, chilled

Wash agar-agar, and soak in water until soft. Drain, and squeeze out water. Add agar-agar to 2 cups water. Bring to boil, add sugar, and stir on low heat until agar-agar dissolves entirely. Remove to a bowl. Add milk and almond extract. Cool to room temperature, then refrigerate until set. Before serving cut in $\frac{1}{2}$-in.-thick diamonds. Transfer to a serving bowl. Add chilled canned fruit salad with syrup, and serve. Serves 4 as a dessert course. Serves 4–8 Chinese style.

Note: Since the strength of gelatin powder varies with the maker, the cook should use the appropriate quantity of a favorite brand to produce 3 cups of firm gelatin. Agar-agar is preferred for texture.

Sweet Red Beans with Gingko Nuts 紅豆白果粥

COLOR: PAGE 36

1 cup small red beans, soaked overnight
1 cup glutinous rice, washed
$\frac{1}{2}$ cup canned gingko nuts, drained
1 cup brown sugar

Wash red beans, add water to cover, bring to boil, and simmer partially covered 40 minutes or until soft. Add rice and gingko nuts to red beans, and simmer partially covered 40 minutes. Add sugar, and cook on low heat until sugar melts. Serve hot. Serves 3 as a dessert course. Serves 3–6 Chinese style.

Note: Regular rice may be substituted for glutinous rice. If regular rice is used, it should be simmered for 20–25 minutes. If the small red beans are not available, the cook may want to experiment with kidney beans or other favorite beans. Canned, sweetened red beans are available at Japanese food shops (see p. 44). This sweet congee is equally delicious if the beans are eliminated.

List of Recipes

Poultry
- Jellied Chicken (鷄　凍)
- Skewered Chicken Livers (炸 鷄 肝)
- Chopped Chicken with Lettuce (炒 鷄 鬆)
- Duck with Chinese Cabbage (紅 燒 鴨)
- Chicken Breast with Pineapple (鷄脯菠菜)
- Braised Chicken with Black Bean Sauce (豆 豉 鷄)
- Braised Duck with Onions (洋 葱 鴨)
- Fried Duck (香 酥 鴨)
- Lemon Chicken (檸 檬 鷄)
- Chicken with Chestnuts (栗 子 鷄)
- Fried Chicken (whole) (脆 皮 鷄)
- Drunk Chicken (醉　鷄)
- Steamed Chicken with Ham (鷄片蒸火腿)
- Sautéed Chicken Livers with Celery (鷄肝炒芹菜)
- Fried Chicken (pieces) (炸 鷄 塊)
- White Chicken (白　鷄)
- Longevity Chicken (枸子淮山鷄)
- Chicken with Walnuts (炒核桃鷄丁)

Fish
- Sweet and Sour Fish (糖 醋 魚)
- Steamed Salmon with Eggs (蛋 蒸 魚)
- Steamed Fish (清 蒸 魚)
- Spiced Fish Slices (燻　魚)
- Braised Fish with Beancurd (砂鍋魚燉豆腐)

Shellfish
- Cold Lobster (竜蝦沙律)
- Spicy Shrimp (塩 焗 蝦)
- Shrimp with Celery (芹菜炒蝦仁)
- Two-Color Shrimp Balls (鴛鴦蝦球)
- Sweet and Sour Prawns (糖醋大蝦)
- Fried Shrimp (清炸蝦仁)
- Sesame Shrimp Toast (芝麻蝦挞)
- Fried Oysters with Asparagus (酥炸生蠔・竜鬚菜)
- Scallops and Chicken Livers with Celery (炒鷄肝芹菜)
- Fried Crab Claws (蟹　角)
- Crab with Black Bean Sauce (豆 豉 蟹)

Jellyfish and Cucumber (海蜇皮拌黃瓜)
Stir-fried Cuttlefish (炒魷魚)

Beef

Ground Beef with Green Peas (牛肉末炒青豆)
Chinese Beef Steak (中式牛排)
Beef with Shredded Potatoes (煎牛肉上豆絲)
Beef with Broccoli (牛肉炒芥蘭)
Stir-Fried Beef with Snow Peas (牛肉炒青豆)
Anise Braised Beef (茴香牛肉)

Pork

Cold Cut Arrangement (冷拼盤)
Pork with Plums (酸梅蒸豬肉)
Fried Pork with Pickles (肉絲炒雪菜)
Barbecued Spareribs (烤大排骨)
Braised Spareribs (醬油烤排骨)
Pork with String Beans (肉燉扁豆角)
Sweet and Sour Pork Strips (醋溜肉条)
Pork with Cucumber (肉片炒黃瓜)
Barbecued Pork (叉燒)
Sausage (臘腸)
Fried Pork (炸肉塊)
Sweet and Sour Pork (古老肉)

Vegetables

Braised Mushrooms with Asparagus (燴草菇竜須菜)
Steamed Stuffed Green Peppers (肉釀青椒)
Marinated Cucumber (鹹黃瓜)
Chili Turnips (辣蘿蔔)
Pickled Red Radishes (醃小紅蘿蔔)
Beauty in Bloom (双花比美)
Beancurd with Oyster Sauce (白菌燴豆腐)
Fried Stuffed Eggplant (炸茄盒)
Steamed Wintermelon with Ham (蒸冬瓜夾)
Stuffed Mushrooms with Sausage (百花斎放)
Corn Fritters (炸玉米)
Spicy Assorted Vegetables (炒素菜)
Braised Assorted Vegetables (冬茹冬筍燴素菜)
Sautéed Beancurd with Mushrooms (紅燒豆腐)
Green Peppers and Bean Sprouts (炒銀芽青椒)
Assorted Vegetables with Black Pickles (炒鹹菜丁)
Spicy Salad (炒素菜)
Chilled Cucumber (涼黃瓜)
Crisp Peanuts (炸花生)
Spicy Lima Beans (五香蚕豆)

Egg

Deep Fried Eggs (翡翠果)
Forest Eggs (木須蛋)
Scrambled Eggs with Crabmeat (蟹肉炒蛋)

Rice, Noodles, and Bread

Fried Rice with Assorted Meat (什錦炒飯)
Abalone and Chicken Congee (鮑魚粥)
Fried Wonton (炸餛飩)
Spring Rolls (炸春卷)
Crisp Fried Noodles with Spinach (菠菜炸麵)
Soft Fried Noodles with Shrimp (蝦仁炒麵)

Egg Noodles (鷄蛋麵)
Spinach Noodles (菠菜麵)
Noodles with Shrimp (蝦仁湯麵)
Noodles with Chicken (鷄絲湯麵)
Steamed Dumplings (蒸餃)
Fried Dumplings (鍋貼)
Shrimp Dumplings (蝦餃)
Steamed Flower Buns (花卷)
Steamed Silver Strand Rolls (銀絲卷)

Soup

Corn Soup with Ground Chicken (鷄茸粟米湯)
Beef in Yunnan Pot (雲南汽鍋牛肉)
Chinese Cabbage and Mushroom Soup (白菜冬茹湯)
Shrimp Ball Soup (蝦丸湯)
Watercress Soup (牛肉西洋菜湯)
Clam Soup (蛤蜊湯)
Cantonese Firepot (火鍋子)

Desserts

Glazed Sweet Potatoes (拔絲白薯)
Stuffed Apples (釀苹果)
Fruit Compote (水果汁)
Stuffed Sweet Lotus (糖蓮藕)
Longan and Lichee Compote (荔枝桂円汁)
Sesame Puffs (炸煎堆)
Almond Float (杏仁豆腐)
Sweet Red Beans with Gingko Nuts (紅豆白果粥)

Index

abalone, 85, 124
   and chicken congee, 106
agar-agar, 42, 59, 129
almond float, 129
anise, star, 43
appetizers
   chicken, jellied, 59
   chicken liver, 60
   cold cuts, 85, 86
   crab claws, 78
   cucumber, 94, 101
   fish slices, 72
   lima beans, spicy, 102
   lobster, 73
   mushrooms, stuffed, 97
   peanuts, fried, 101
   radishes, pickled, 95
   shrimp balls, 75
   shrimp, spicy, 74
   shrimp toast, 76
   spring rolls, 107
   turnips, chili, 94
   wonton, fried, 106
apples, stuffed, 126
asparagus
   mushrooms with, 93
   oysters with, 77

bamboo shoots, 43, 121
bean(s)
   black fermented, 44
      chicken with, 62
      crab with, 79
   lima, 102
   red, 44
      with gingko nuts, 129
   string, pork with, 89
bean sprouts, 43
   and green peppers, 100
beancurd, 43, 124
   fish with, 71
   with mushrooms, 99
   with oyster sauce, 96
beef, 96, 122, 124
   anise braised, 84
   with broccoli, 83
   with green peas, 81
   liver, 124
   with shredded potatoes, 82
   with snow peas, 83
   stewed, 121
   steak, Chinese, 82
bowls, 55, 56
bread, steamed, 116, 119
broccoli,
   beef with, 83
   and cauliflower with crab roe, 95
buns, steamed, 116

cabbage, pickled, 88

cauliflower and broccoli with crab
  roe, 95
celery
  scallops and chicken livers with,
    66, 77
  shrimp with, 74
chestnuts, chicken with, 64
chicken, 124
  and abalone congee, 106
  with black bean sauce, 62
  boiled, 68
  breast, 61, 85, 113
  with chestnuts, 64
  corn soup with, 120
  drunk, 65
  fried, 65, 67
  jellied, 59
  lemon, 64
  and lettuce, 60
  livers, 60, 66, 77
  soup stock, 48
  steamed, 66
  with walnuts, 68
  white, 67
Chinese cabbage, 44, 124
  duck with, 61
  and mushroom soup, 121
chopping, fine, 53
chopsticks, 56
chün shan wafers, 68

clam soup, 123
cold cuts, 85, 86
compote
  fruit, 126
  longan and lichee, 127
congee, abalone and chicken, 106
cooking styles, regional, 40
corn fritters, 98
corn soup with chicken, 120
crab(s)
  with black bean sauce, 79
  claws, fried, 78
  roe, cauliflower and broccoli
    with, 95
crabmeat
  balls, 124
  scrambled eggs with, 104
cucumber, 86
  chilled, 101
  jellyfish and, 79
  marinated, 94
  pork with, 90
cuttlefish, 124
  stir-fried, 80
cutting board, 41

dicing, 53
deep frying, 55
duck
  braised, with onions, 62

  with Chinese cabbage, 61
  fried, 63
dumplings
  fried, 115
  shrimp, 115
  steamed, 114

egg(s)
  with cloud ear mushrooms, 104
  deep fried, 103
  quail, 44
  raw, 124
  salmon with, 70
  scrambled, with crabmeat, 104
  yolk, steamed, 86
egg noodles, 108
eggplant, 44
  stuffed, 96

firepot, Cantonese, 123
fish, 124
  with beancurd, 71
  spiced, 72
  steamed, 70
  sweet and sour, 69
five-flavor spice, 44
flour, glutinous rice, 44
fritters, corn, 98
fruit
  compote, 126

salad, 129

gelatin, 42, 59, 129
ginger, fresh, 44
ginko nuts, 44
    red beans with, 129
green peas, beef with, 81
green pepper(s)
    and bean sprouts, 100
    stuffed, 94

ham, 85
    chicken with, 66
    wintermelon with, 97
hoisin sauce, 45

jellyfish
    and cucumber, 79
    dried, 45

knives, 41
kou tzu seeds, 68

leek, 45
lemon chicken, 64
lettuce, chicken with, 60
lichee, 45
    and longan compote, 127
lily root, 45, 126
lima beans, spicy, 102

liver
    beef, 124
    chicken, 60, 66, 77
lobster, cold, 73
longan, 45
    and lichee compote, 127
lotus root, 45
    stuffed, 127
lotus seeds, 45, 126

meat, assorted, fried rice with, 105
mushroom(s), 121
    with asparagus, 93
    beancurd with, 99
    braised, 86
    dried Chinese, 45
    soup, and Chinese cabbage, 121
    stuffed, 97
    white, 93, 96, 99
mushrooms, cloud ear, 46, 90
    eggs with, 104
noodles
    with chicken, 113
    dried Chinese, 46
    eggs, 108
    fried
        with shrimp, 108
        with spinach, 107
    with shrimp, 114
    spinach, 113

oil, 46
    red pepper, 46
    sesame, 46
onions, duck with, 62
oranges, mandarin, 126
oysters, 124
    fried, 77
oyster sauce, 46
    beancurd with, 96

pans, 41
pastry, sesame, 128
peanuts, fried, 101
pepper, anise, 47
    red chili, 47
pepper-salt mixture, 47
pineapple, 126
    chicken breast with, 61
pickles
    black, assorted vegetables with, 100
    pork with, 88
plates, 55
plums, preserved, 47
    pork with, 87
pork, 79, 94, 96, 97, 99, 100, 107, 114, 115, 121, 124
    barbecued, 85, 90
    with cucumber, 90
    fried, 91

   with pickles, 88
   with plums, 87
   sausage, 91
   with string beans, 89
   sweet and sour, 89, 92
   tripe, 124
potatoes, shredded, 82
prawns, sweet and sour, 75

radishes, pickled, 95
rice, 47
   flour, glutinous, 44
   fried, 105
   glutinous, 47, 126, 129
rolls, steamed, 119
rose wine, 47

salad, spicy, 101
salmon, steamed, 70
sausage, pork, 91
   stuffed mushrooms with, 97
scallops, 66, 77, 124
scoring, 54
sesame puffs, 128
shredding, 53
shrimp, 78, 97, 106, 114, 115, 124
   balls, 75, 124
   ball soup, 122
   with celery, 74
   dumplings, 115
   fried, 76
   noodles with, 108, 114
   spicy, 74
   toast, 76
slicing, 53
snow peas, beef with, 83
soup
   beef, 121, 122
   Chinese cabbage and mushroom, 121
   clam, 123
   corn, with chicken, 120
   shrimp ball, 122
   stock, 48
   watercress, 122
soup spoons, 56
soy sauce, 48
spareribs
   barbecued, 88
   braised, 88, 89
spinach, 124
   noodles, 113
   noodles with, 107
spring rolls, 107
steak, Chinese beef, 82
steamer, 42
steaming, 55
stir-frying, 54
strawberries, 126
string beans, pork with, 89

sweet and sour
   fish, 69
   pork, 89, 92
   prawns, 75
sweet potatoes, glazed, 125
Szechwan pickles, 88

teacups, 56
toast, shrimp, 76
tongue, 85
tripe, pork, 124
turnips, chili, 94

vermicelli, transparent, 48, 124
vegetables, assorted
   with black pickles, 100
   braised, 99
   spicy, 98

walnuts, chicken with, 68
water chestnuts, 48, 126
watercress soup, 122
wedging, 54
wine, 47, 48
wintermelon, 48
   with ham, 97
wok, 41, 42
wonton, fried, 106

Yunnan pot, beef in, 121

定価1,500円